PREACHING AND THE NON-ORDAINED

PREACHING
and the
NON-ORDAINED

An Interdisciplinary Study

Edited by
Nadine Foley, O.P.

THE LITURGICAL PRESS

Collegeville

Minnesota

Library of Congress Cataloging in Publication Data

Main entry under title:

Preaching and the non-ordained.

Delivered at a symposium sponsored by the Dominican Leadership Conference in Columbus, Ohio, Oct. 8–10, 1982.

1. Preaching, Lay — Congresses.   I. Foley, M. Nadine, 1924–   II. Dominican Leadership Conference.

BV4235.L3P73   1983   251   83-7963

ISBN 0-8146-1291-1 (pbk.)

Contents

PREACHING AND THE NON-ORDAINED

Introduction

NADINE FOLEY, O.P.

The period through which the American Churches are passing is one in which more and more Christian people are coming to a mature faith. They seek not a mere passive presence to the rites and ministries of institutional religion but a vital, active participation, both in public worship and in the Churches' mission to the world. Ours is a personalistic social milieu in which people are conscious of their individual gifts and are motivated to use those gifts appropriately and responsibly. It is a particularly promising time for the Church as a people of God called individually and corporately to become fully alive in the redeeming experience of Jesus Christ.

For the Roman Catholic Church, the new self-awareness of its members offers challenge and opportunity. But the consistently recurring question in a number of areas revolves around the issue of whether or not the inherited structures and practices are adaptable to the needs and aspirations of contemporary Catholics and adequate to the task of proclaiming the gospel at what appears to be a critical turning point of human history. One of the questions being raised pertains to preaching, a function currently authorized to be carried out in the liturgical setting by bishops, priests, and deacons. But can preaching be done within the Christian assembly by those who are not ordained? The question goes beyond mere juridical considerations to encompass concerns for the rights of Christians and for the evident charisms that exist among them.

Experience shows that ordination does not infallibly confer the gift of effective preaching. It shows further, in many places where non-ordained persons are preaching, that the gift for preaching is widely distributed among the Church's members, and especially among women and men who are actively meeting the many demands of today's ministries.

When thoughtful people reflect upon the situation, it becomes evident that little formal study of the office of preaching, its historical development, and its presumed integral relation to the role of the priest in the celebration of the Eucharist has been done. This fact became particularly evident to American Dominican men and women, members of the Order of Preachers, who have new reasons to assess the meaning of the Order's charism, shared by both its ordained and non-ordained members, as they participate in the movements of the present time. Women members of the Order especially have persistent questions about their identity as *preachers* in the light of their own new claims upon full personhood supported both by society and the message of the gospel. It was to address the emerging questions that the Dominican Leadership Conference in 1975 established a special commission to examine and report on issues related to Dominican women and preaching.

That commission* first produced a paper, "Unless They Be Sent: A Theological Report on Dominican Women Preaching," for study and reflection by the women's congregations, the provinces of men, and the Dominican laity. Subsequently, a new standing commission was established to continue the exploration. To this group it became clear that the concerns that had motivated their work in a very particular way were shared by many others in the Church in a more general way. The Dominican Leadership Conference then authorized the commission to plan a special conference on preaching by the non-ordained to be developed in an interdisciplinary mode and to be open to all interested persons. This volume contains the papers that formed

---

*Composed of Dominicans Diana Culbertson, Marie Walter Flood, Dorothy Folliard, Louise Hageman, Thomas O'Meara, and Lucy Vasquez.

the core of the discussions held at that event in Columbus, Ohio, October 8–10, 1982.

In bringing the conference on Preaching and the Non-Ordained to reality, the work of Kathleen Cannon, O.P., who chaired the commission, was persistent and unstinting. Similarly, the commission members — Joan Delaplane, O.P., Diane Kennedy, O.P., Joseph Konkel, O.P., and Robert Perry, O.P. — contributed the indispensable work and resources that made the conference possible. As liaison between them and the Dominican Leadership Conference, I wish to acknowledge their contribution. I am personally grateful to Mary Francis McDonald, O.P., Jennifer Shipley Langner, Karen Payer, and Carolyn Hilles-Plant for their sharing the work of preparing the manuscript for publication. In addition, I want to express special appreciation for the expertise and editorial care provided by John Schneider of The Liturgical Press.

Opening Remarks

KATHLEEN CANNON, O.P.

"When the Spirit of truth comes, he will guide you into all the truth; for he will not speak on his own authority, but whatever he hears he will speak, and he will declare to you the things that are to come" (John 16:13).

As Christians, we proclaim our belief in the abiding presence of the Holy Spirit in the community, as immanent to the believing community. The Spirit of Jesus is present, active, living within us. As the heart of the Church, the Spirit is the principle of life and vitality for the community. It is the Spirit who is the source of the prophetic nature of the Christian community. The Spirit guides through human structures and, at least in principle, there is no opposition between the Spirit and the Church, between the Spirit's work and our work. One index of this direction by the Spirit is the gradual arising within the Church of new questions that are resolved through discussion and human exchange, from which the Spirit is not absent. For the Spirit's work, while transcendent, occurs in and through the human experiences of evaluating, trying, testing, asking, studying, discussing.

The matter of this particular conference, namely, preaching by the non-ordained, is one that has come forth within Christian circles. In fact and in spontaneous experience, women and lay men are being asked or "called" to the ministry of preaching, either occasionally or regularly. Further, they are being called even by designated leaders of the Christian community. There are those, too, who have discerned a charism for preaching and

7

who claim that they are able truly to mediate the gospel of Christ to contemporary Christian communities on the basis of their own gospel experience.

On the other hand, the non-ordained are also being denied opportunities to preach. We do not lack for examples, both written and hearsay, of a lay person being directed to speak at a time other than the homily or their words referred to as a "meditation or reflection." At the same time, there are groups within the Church calling for an extension of the situations in which it is permissible for non-ordained persons to preach. Both the Canon Law Society of America and the Dominican Leadership Conference of the United States have been working to this end and have invested time, expertise, and scholarship toward uprooting stubborn residual problems in key areas of the theology of preaching. These are all indicators of rising practical changes and mounting theoretical concerns in regard to all forms of the preaching of the gospel by qualified baptized lay persons.

While we are certainly not the first to ask who may preach the gospel with authority in the midst of the ecclesial assembly, nevertheless there is a certain newness or urgency to the question today. The newness derives from our understanding of the ecclesial nature of the laity, their status as members of God's people and sharers in the salvific mission of the Church. It emerges, too, from the contemporary discussion of the role of women: the existential reality of who women are in general society and therefore in the society of the historical Church is not the same as it has been throughout much of Christian history. Finally, our heightened awareness of the need for evangelization and the new milieu of preaching—the demands that our times place for preaching the Word—underscore the need for a general revitalization of preaching. The questions put to us today call upon us to pay the price of this grace by serious theological reflection, carried out in an atmosphere of prayer. This matter, then, is an issue of truly ecclesial concern for all members of the Church—men and women, lay and ordained—for the essential reality before us all is that of preaching the Word of God and how we can best do that in our age.

The matter needs to be faced; to fail to do so would be to fail the challenges inherent in belief. The question arises from faith and demands an answer in faith. It is no Christian solution to bury one's head in the sand. The matter of lay preaching calls for open, honest, theological and ecclesiological reflection and diagnosis to find out what is from the Spirit, to "hold fast what is good, abstain from every form of evil" (1 Thess 5:21-22).

Hence this gathering of learned and committed believers is convened to open up the parameters of the question in an irenic atmosphere. There are multiple facets to the question; we hope to illuminate some. Our intention is to provide some clarity around the issue of ordained/non-ordained preaching from biblical, theological, historical, and juridical perspectives. And so the presentations will be concerned with the data of the Scriptures, theological reflection, the Christian tradition, ecclesial law, and liturgy.

We invited Father Schillebeeckx because of the dedication he has shown throughout his scholarly life to the practical and pastoral side of things. While he is Belgian, from a basically French culture, and one that is rather speculative, he has adapted himself to the very practical kind of Christianity found in Holland. He has consistently worked with the Dutch bishops in dealing with problems of an ecclesiastical kind, besides dealing with questions such as marriage, chastity, religious life in the contemporary world, the lay person in the Church, and so on. The point is, of course, that without sacrificing any of his philosophical and theological learning, he has never been an ivory-tower, merely professional theologian.

The Right of Every Christian to Speak in the Light of Evangelical Experience "In the Midst of Brothers and Sisters"

EDWARD SCHILLEBEECKX, O.P.

The various theologies of the Church's official ministries, including that of the preaching office, do not originate in a vacuum. They come about for the most part in a struggle for authority, in a process involving the formation of "roles" in a group or community and as part of system differentiation, frequently even as a justification of historically acquired positions of power or monopoly. From the sociological point of view, this is what happens in all group formation, not excluding the formation of that community we call the "community of God" or the "Church."

If this whole context of group formation and group differentiation is not borne in mind in our theological reflection, we cannot properly assess the true evangelical value of any obligatory "theological substance." Furthermore, we are unable to evaluate appropriately the authority and the importance of the Church's official pronouncements on issues such as the prohibition of lay preaching. In short, without the sociological dimension we risk being exposed to pure ideology.

11

In our interpretation of the Church's pronouncements, including those about the preaching office, it is important to recognize that the theology of the Church's office has always been formulated by those who are in office and who, generally speaking, oppose any new ideas expressed by Christians that deviate from their own. Concretely, this means that the history of the theology of office, including the prohibition of preaching by lay persons, has been a history of official ecclesiastical triumph, in which the vanquished have been marginalized or even completely silenced. What has developed historically in such instances is then customarily described as "divine justice"!

We must therefore analyze the Church's statements about the right and authority to preach if we are to grasp the implications of their obligatory "theological substance." We must be critical of ideology and bear in mind the socio-historical contexts of the varying theologies of office.

If, then, we are to interpret correctly the evangelical meaning and implications of this prohibition within the Church, we must have a clear historical insight into the development of the Church's preaching, and therefore into the situations in the Church and the world within which the Church proclaimed its prohibition of lay preaching. I shall therefore provide a brief survey of the history of the Middle Ages, when preaching by lay people was banned for the first time in the history of the Church. The emergence of what in the Middle Ages was called the Dominican *Praedicatio Jesu Christi* was of special historical importance not only at the time but also generally in the Church here and now, in connection with the position in the Church of those of us who are Dominicans.

I. The Revival of Lay Preaching and the Church's Reaction

From the ninth century onward, the proclamation of the gospel was one of the functions of local parish priests or leaders of local communities. In the early Church, catechesis (the catechumenate) had been in the hands of both priests and lay deacons. In the Middle Ages, however, preaching and catechesis gradually came to be more and more closely connected with the celebration of the Eucharist on Sunday, and consequently with the church building. As a result, the focus shifted to the parish clergy, who were responsible for the pastoral care of the people. Proclamation therefore gradually became synonymous with priestly preaching, and even with preaching linked to the diocese.

The great expansion of the monastic abbeys in the Middle Ages threatened this traditional diocesan and parochial pastoral care. These abbeys, which did not themselves have parishes, soon became centers of pastoral care, with the result that there were many clashes between the parochial and the abbatial centers. At the beginning of this struggle, all the national councils and synods defended the parish structure of pastoral care and insisted that monastic pastoral care had to be integrated into the diocesan and parochial context.

These Church regulations were preceded by lengthy polemics. The issues revolved around the fact that monks, most of whom were not priests and were therefore in that sense laymen, began to preach and attract large audiences. The Church's ultimate prohibition against the preaching of these non-ordained monks was, from the historical point of view, based on the need to protect the diocesan and parochial structure. It was, in other words, an expression of the Church's opposition to the emancipation of monastic pastoral care from the diocesan context. The consequence of this Church opposition was that, in the tenth and eleventh centuries, all the great abbeys neglected the pastoral care of those who lived in the neighborhood, leaving it to the diocesan clergy.

Gregory the Great had already laid the foundations for this system in A.D. 591 in his well-known *Liber regulae pastoralis*,[1] a book that was later to be the inspiration for the entire medieval spirituality of the preaching office. The author's point of departure was that preaching was the sole right of bishops, who possessed the fullness of the pastoral office and formed the *ordo praedicatorum*, that is, the order or body of preachers.

This system was based on the hierarchical distinction made between "the higher" and "the lower," that is, between leadership and obedience. At that time, communication was quite one-sided and went from above to below. The Church had taken over the social and political models of authority from Roman culture, which was declining at that time, and these provided the framework for the whole organization of the Church's life. Believers were subject to the *imperium praedicatorum*, and preaching thus became a form of rule. *Praedicatio* (preaching) and *praelatio* (being a "prelate" or, in other words, a "superior") thus became essentially linked with one another. Women above all were excluded from the office of preaching, because they were, in this early phase of feudalism, subject to men. It is clear, however, that this exclusion was based, not on woman's nature, but rather on her subordinate position. An abbess, insofar as she was *superior*, that is, the "superior" of a community, had the right to proclaim the Word of God to her "subjects," even if there were men among them.

As the "order of preachers," the bishops were regarded as the successors of the twelve apostles. The parish clergy, on the other hand, were viewed as the successors of the seventy-two disciples sent by Jesus. This interpretation led parish priests to develop a quasi-episcopal form of spirituality, since they possessed the right to preach by virtue of being sent by their bishops. Their pastoral office was linked to an episcopal *foedus*, or land held in fee (a "benefice"), with the result that the relationship between the bishop and his parish clergy was similar to that between a feudal lord and his vassals. Only the pastors — the bishops and their clergy — were the "light of the world." Lay people were simply their subjects and the objects of their priestly pastoral care.

This traditional medieval organization of the Church was shaken in the eleventh century by all kinds of new phenomena. Many new religious orders originated at this time; heretics — and especially laymen — went around preaching; parish priests lived in community as "canons regular"; and the investiture controversy between *sacerdotium* and *imperium,* the pope and the emperor, came to a head. Preaching as a whole began to become dissociated from the traditional type of territorially organized "pastoral office."

The main aim of the Gregorian reform was to bring the secularized parish clergy back to a genuine evangelical ministry, and in so doing to make preaching part of the effort to reform the Church. Ordinary believers everywhere were violently opposed to "unworthy priests," and above all to the administration of the sacraments by such priests. Even monks preached against the general decadence of the diocesan clergy, with the result that popes imposed a ban on preaching by monks, most of whom were laymen.[2] Formerly, lay people had been forbidden to preach because, due to their lack of education, they were prone to propagating heresy and to giving scandal. Now, however, it was said: Only priests may preach; monks and laymen may not, "however well educated they may be."[3] This proscription was a reaction to the sharp criticism made by monks and lay people about the secular clergy, who had become very worldly, and about the structure of the Church. It was not really a theological position taken up against lay preaching, but rather a defense of the management of pastoral care within the Church.

There were, however, popes who defended preaching by monks and laymen because the latter supported their programs of reform against reluctant bishops and diocesan priests. As a result, the people were, in a sense, emancipated from the prevailing structures of the Church, and their emancipation was supported by popes, who tried by this means to increase their rights of primacy over the bishops.

In the course of these polemics, Pope Gregory VII gave permission to individual priests and also to groups of priests for supra-diocesan preaching. Preachers were thereby given a kind of exemption from the jurisdiction of the local bishops. The first papal permission to preach without the permission of the local bishop was granted in 1122 by Pope Callistus II to a Flemish monk of the Abbey of Saint Peter in Ghent, in modern Belgium. The monks there "happened" to support the Pope against the policy of the emperor!

Nonetheless, there was no real deviation from the principle that preaching was a priestly function. Preaching, however, was at this time often used, with papal approval, as an instrument in the hands of monk-priests against territorially restricted pastoral care, which disregarded the papal reform decrees. In this way, a new type of preacher emerged—the *praedicator publicus*, or "public preacher," a priest provided by Rome with the power to preach, regardless of what local bishops thought of this practice. Priestly members of religious orders thus became the pope's shock troops against the bishops who were reluctant to implement the reform decrees.

The situation gave rise to continued conflict between the monks and the canons regular. The latter favored reform that would bar monk-priests with no parish duties from preaching the gospel. The controversy was eventually settled when both groups accepted the principle that the right to preach was based, not on a papal or episcopal "mission," but on the sacrament of ordination as such. This resolution amounted to a complete change in the theology of the preaching office. The arguments put forward at the time in favor of the right to proclaim the gospel are therefore extremely significant:

1. Certain theologians maintained, on the basis of the New Testament, that the right to proclaim the gospel was to be found in the *vita apostolica,* that is, in the imitation of Jesus in an evangelical way or praxis of life, and that it was this praxis that gave a person the right to bear witness through preaching.

2. Others based this right on the *missio*, the fact that one was "sent" by the local bishop or the supra-diocesan pope.

3. Still others believed that the right to preach was based on the *ordo clericorum* (the clerical rank), or at least on the acceptance of the clerical state by receiving the order of tonsure.

4. Finally, there were theologians who thought that the right to preach was based exclusively on priestly ordination as such. Both monks and canons regular appealed initially to the *vita apostolica*, however, as the basis for all authority to preach.

There was, therefore, in the twelfth century, a movement away from the traditional link between pastoral care (the *cura animarum*, or "care of souls," with the right to a prebend) and preaching, and toward a new connection between priestly ordination and preaching. This was the result of the compromise reached in the conflict between the monks and the canons regular. The monks recognized that they had no other chance of providing a legitimate basis for their own right to preach the gospel as opposed to that of the canons, who were vested with parochial office. The ultimate consequence of this compromise was, therefore, the clericalization of the preaching office.

The right to proclaim the gospel, which, through the medium of pastoral care, had previously been concerned with people in a definite parish, thus became in the twelfth century an abstract privilege enjoyed by "ordained" men and dissociated from a specific parish community. It became, in other words, a sign of the difference between the priest and the lay person. At the same time, it became dissociated from pastoral duties.

The immediate consequence of this movement was that those who were not ordained, that is, lay people, were declared incompetent to preach. Because of polemics among the clergy, then, there was a radical break with the earlier charismatic and missionary tradition, which had led to the Christianization of the whole of Europe through the proclamation of the gospel by Irish and Scottish monks, most of whom had not been priests. Now monks went against that earlier basis of their preaching function and were forced by the polemics with the canons regular to base their right to preach on priestly ordination also. From this time onward it was accepted that "mitti est ordinari," in the words of Rupert of Deutz.[4] As a principle, priestly ordination in itself became the *missio canonica* for the authority to preach.

In this conflict between monks and canons, the lay person was not essentially involved. What was at stake was the emancipation of the secular clergy from the early medieval supremacy of the monks, and therefore the maintenance of a plurality of forms of life within the organization of the Church. The historical link between the authority to preach and the clerical status (the position of the canons regular) or even between the authority to preach and priestly ordination (the position of the Benedictine monks especially) was therefore the result of a competitive struggle among the clergy.

In the period that followed, this struggle led to an essential restriction in the latitude allowed to preaching and a limitation upon what was theologically both possible and legitimate. This conclusion is clear from the fact that in the second half of the twelfth century, an appeal made by a lay person to the *Statuta Ecclesiae antiqua*, according to which lay persons too were permitted to preach, had no effect at all. By this time it had been canonically decreed that preaching was the exclusive right of priests. The monks who, in light of the ancient charisma, might have been able to defend the laity here defaulted. The peace that they concluded with the canons, on the basis of their common priesthood, led to a sharper delineation of the preaching office, and lay preaching was from this time onward seen as a usurpation of clerical powers.

We arrive, therefore, at a first theological conclusion. The refusal of the medieval Church to allow lay people to preach in public had in fact no theological foundation. In other words, it was not based on the essential being of Christian communities, with their multiplicity of ministries; it was rather the result of

(a) a competitive struggle among the clergy for the preaching office; (b) general alarm brought about by heretical propaganda, spread mainly by lay people; and (c) the medieval view of the lay person as illiterate or uneducated — in other words, as *vir saecularis* ("secular man"), who was exclusively concerned with worldly and not Church affairs and who was subordinate in the whole Christian world *(Christianitas,* understood as the Church).

There were popes, Innocent III especially, who tried to rescue lay preaching by making a distinction between *exhortatio* (bearing witness to faith as evangelical encouragement) and *praedicatio* (preaching), which was restricted to priests because it presupposed a knowledge of Scripture. Even Innocent III, however, proposed this division within the context of his Church policy promoting papal supremacy over the local bishops, who were being severely criticized by lay people.

II. THE EMERGENCE AND THE SIGNIFICANCE OF THE DOMINICAN PRAEDICATIO JESU CHRISTI

1. The First Version of the Dominican Ideal of the Preacher

Pope Innocent III (1198–1216) wanted to launch a general campaign against heresies and to include in this effort lay people, subject to the guidance of priests. His intention was that this new crusade of preaching would be carried out by a supraregional body of preachers. They were to be sent out to people under the instructions of the Pope himself and not of the local bishops. What he had in mind, then, was a preaching campaign carried out by a specialized body of preachers, or an *ordo praedicatorum.*

Initially the entire plan misfired. It gained direction only after Diego, the Spanish bishop of Osma, and Dominic Guzman, superior of his cathedral chapter, encountered in Montpellier the first band of preachers, composed primarily of Cistercians. Bishop Diego's diagnosis was that the preaching campaign had failed because the preachers themselves had not adopted the simple and very poor way of life of the apostolic groups of heretics.

Innocent III supported this view of the situation and, under the guidance of Bishop Diego, a second and even bigger mission, called the *Praedicatio Jesu Christi*, was organized to preach to the heretics in the very center of heretical activity at that time, the region between Toulouse and Carcassonne. Apart from Dominic, all the preachers were Cistercians. All came from areas outside the diocese, and none enjoyed the support of the local clergy. This specialized body of preachers divided the entire region up among the members. Bishop Diego and Dominic made Prouille, a place between Fanjeaux and Montréal, the center for their preaching. With the help of a number of pious women, they built a kind of hospice there as a base from which the preachers could go out into the surrounding countryside. In this they were following the tactics of the Cathari, the ascetic initiates of the heretical sect.

Bishop Diego died on December 30, 1207, and Dominic became the leader of the movement. The name *Praedicatio Jesu Christi* was transferred to the apostolic headquarters in Prouille. The Albigensian war broke out at this time, and the papal legate was murdered in 1208. Because Toulouse became the center of the war, Dominic withdrew to Prouille for five years. Very little is known about the events that took place up to 1209, although we do know that it was generally believed at the Council of Avignon in 1209 that the virulent heresy could be effectively combated only if cooperation with the local bishop and his diocesan clergy was strengthened. The "papal exemption" of the preachers in relation to the local clergy had apparently turned out to be ill-advised, and the diocese itself had to be actively involved in combating the heresy.[5]

After the war, on April 25, 1214, Toulouse was set free from its second interdict, and its bishop, Fulk, returned to the city with his clergy after an absence of three years. He called Dominic, among others, to Toulouse. A year later, in 1215, several Christians there took the vow of an order and joined Dominic. This was the beginning of the Dominican Order as an *Ordo Praedicatorum*, holding the first place of "diocesan right." In June, 1215, this body of preachers was established and authorized by the local bishop in these words: "The bishop appoints Brother Dominic and his brethren in his diocese to drive out the heresy by proclaiming the true Christian faith and sound ethics. The preachers are to adopt the way of life of a religious order, and they are to follow the *vita apostolica*, going around on foot proclaiming the gospel and living themselves in evangelical poverty. The diocese is to provide this 'Order of Preaching Brethren' with a financial basis."[6]

It is clear, then, that the *Praedicatio Jesu Christi* began as a supra-diocesan mission that was initially sanctioned by the Pope and soon became a specialized body of preachers working on a diocesan basis among both believers and unbelievers. There was, in this initial Dominican foundation, a certain compromise between the papally exempt definition of the aim of the mission, which goes back to Pope Innocent III,[7] and the economic and jurisdictional placing of the *Ordo Praedicatorum* within a diocesan context, a measure recommended by the Council of Avignon.

The Order of Preachers was initially an order of clergy, priests and helpers of the local bishop, and was not part of the parochial context. Its members were sent out and remunerated by the bishop from the tithes of the diocese. This kind of independent and specialized body of preachers, which nonetheless belonged to the local bishop, was, by comparison with the traditional mode of pastoral care and preaching, something completely new. Preaching was dissociated from the office of leadership of the parochial community and entrusted to a specialized body, whose members were theologically trained in the local chapter school of Saint Etienne.[8]

This new model of preaching brethren contained significant innovations. (a) In the first place, the ministry of preaching was no longer tied to the parish and was not restricted to combating heresy. The power to preach extended over the whole territory of the diocese.[9] When Dominic went to Rome in 1216 to have his *Ordo Praedicatorum* approved by the Pope on the basis of the Rule of Saint Augustine, the Dominican idea of preaching throughout the whole diocese was already firmly established.

b) What was especially new in the order of preaching brethren was the episcopal instruction to the whole brotherhood to preach, with the result that future members of the order *ipso facto* had authority to preach. In other words, the order itself was entrusted with the Church's mission to preach. This model was given full recognition at the Fourth Lateran Council, even though there was a departure from the diocesan principle in the later development of the order.

The Fourth Lateran Council took place in 1215. At the council, Pope Innocent III placed his twenty-year policy of Church reform before the bishops. The council said that the ministry of preaching was first and foremost the task of the bishops, but because so many bishops were neglecting this ministry, the council imposed on them the serious obligation of providing a body of preachers who would take care of preaching in their stead. For their part, the bishops were to provide for the maintenance of those preachers.[10]

The Toulouse model of preaching brethren provided by Dominic was thus advocated in principle for all dioceses. It was seen as a kind of functional mission for pastoral care by means of specialized preaching at the diocesan level, even though it was supra-parochial. The intent, then, was to designate a mobile group of preachers recruited from the canonical clergy of the cathedral and capitular churches. Because preaching with heretics in view meant the provision of the sacrament of penance, the only persons who could be considered as members of these supra-parochial bodies of preachers were priests.

It is clear, then, that the charter of Toulouse, bearing witness to the first Dominican foundation six months before the Fourth Lateran Council, was the intermediary between the decree of Avignon and that of the Lateran Council. The council, however, went much further than the local synod of Avignon in one respect and was almost word for word in agreement with the Dominican charter of Toulouse, namely, that an *Ordo Praedicatorum* should assist the bishop in the context of the whole diocese.

What was also new here was the provision that recruitment should be made mainly from the canons regular, that is, from clergy following a religious rule of life. (Dominic himself had originally been a member of the canons regular and had insisted that his preachers follow their type of rule.) Also new was the extension of the authority to preach to include the administration of the sacrament of penance, according to the model in the *Praedicatio Jesu Christi* of Toulouse and its reconciliatory activity. The sacrament of penance was not linked in the abstract with the authority to preach; the two were connected historically and in the concrete. The proclamation of conversion is by its very nature linked with the ministry of reconciliation, and therefore with the sacrament of penance.[11]

The local bishops, however, were reluctant and lacking in interest, with the result that there was no direct response to this council. Furthermore, neither the Dominicans nor the Friars Minor saw the council as an invitation to prepare and organize themselves at the diocesan level, and they continued to develop their work in a supra-diocesan context.

According to canon 13 of the Fourth Lateran Council, no new monastic orders were to be founded unless they adopted an existing rule.[12] At the diocesan level, the Dominican Order had already been approved.[13] There was no problem at all here. From the historical point of view, this prohibition was apparently inserted by the bishops, who rejected the papal policy in this matter. During the council the abbots especially were critical of the new Dominican and Franciscan movement, and many of the bishops did not agree with the Pope in his attempt to reconcile the heretics and the lay preachers. Innocent III was, however, able to protect the Franciscans from this conciliar verdict against the new religious orders by approving Francis's rule before the conciliar decrees came into force.[14]

The Lateran decree was directed against the Pope, who, on the basis of the distinction between *exhortatio* (or *disputatio*) and *praedicatio*, aimed at giving some latitude within the Church to the reconciled groups, such as the Humiliati and the Waldenses. The papal concessions on lay preaching were thus an "exceptional law" and not a general law approved by the council. All the same, the general statement "No one other than priests may preach," taken from a letter by Leo the Great, was toned down by canonical tradition through the addition of an early gloss from the *Statuta Ecclesiae antiqua:* "unless with the permission of the priest." Canonists have also pointed to the fact that lay persons belonging to the Orders of Knights Templar and Knights Hospitalers were permitted to preach on the basis of a privilege.[15]

The general tendency in the Western Church was quite clear: the intention was to integrate the supra-diocesan groups of preachers, who were acting by virtue of papal power, into the traditional pastoral structures of the dioceses. It was, however, only during the pontificate of the succeeding pope, Honorius III, that Dominic was able to carry out his original plan.

2. Dominican Preaching as a Specialized, Supra-diocesan Body of Preachers

In 1216, a year after the Fourth Lateran Council, Dominic returned to Rome. On December 22 of that year, Pope Honorius III confirmed the foundation of the brethren of Saint-Romains in Toulouse as a community of Augustinian canons regular. A few weeks later, however, Dominic, with the help of Cardinal

Ugolino, obtained approval of his original idea. As a foundation of Augustinian canons regular, the new order was approved by the Pope as the *Praedicatio Jesu Christi.*[16]

In a letter dated January 21, 1217, in relation to the successor of the bishop of Toulouse, Dominic's position was safeguarded by the Pope. In 1217, Dominic had a conversation in Rome with the bishop of Lund. After this meeting Dominic acted against the advice of the bishop and some of his companions, and did away with the monastery of Saint-Romains. He sent his followers out in pairs to Paris, Spain, Rome, and Bologna, while only a small remnant remained behind in Prouille and Saint-Romains.[17] He obviously wanted to give his order a supra-diocesan status. When he next went to Rome, he achieved his aim, with the help of Cardinal Ugolino. On February 11, 1218, the Pope asked all the bishops and abbots to support the "brethren of the *Ordo Praedicatorum*" and to receive them out of respect for the pope's authority. The papal letter stated that these preaching brethren followed a life of evangelical poverty and proclaimed the gospel without claiming any recompense.[18]

All this was simply a recommendation, but it is apparent from this letter that Dominic did not think of his order as a community of canons regular in the old style, but saw it as a religious order of preaching brothers directly subject to papal authority — a brotherhood of apostolic poverty at the service of the gospel and its proclamation in the whole Church. This was clearly something quite new in relation to the movement of canons regular.

These papal bulls were followed by many others in which the Pope asked the bishops to grant free access to the Dominican preaching brethren wherever they went.[19] The Dominican Order, which had been a diocesan body of specialized preachers, had now become supra-diocesan. Papal recommendations of this type ceased after Dominic's death. They were frequent, however, during the pontificate of Cardinal Ugolino, elected pope in 1227 with the name of Gregory IX. It seems clear that the initiative was taken, then, not by the previous Pope, but by Dominic himself and his protector Ugolino.

On April 26, 1218, Pope Honorius III wrote to all the bishops that they had a duty to receive the preaching brethren and to "allow them to carry out the preaching office that they had been declared competent to execute."[20]

In this way the Dominican Order, as an Order, obtained the right to proclaim the gospel in the whole Church. Strengthened by this authority, Dominic traveled throughout Europe and chose, as centers from which this supra-diocesan preaching should spread, the university cities of Paris and Bologna, which at the time were the two greatest centers of spiritual and intellectual life in Europe. Dominic made sure that his appearance was always backed by papal recommendations.

These papal letters differed in purport from one another, but it is possible to distinguish three basic types. Some of them emphasized the poverty practiced by the preaching brethren, and their intention was clearly to promote the foundation of new Dominican communities in various districts. The bishops were urged to encourage believers to listen to the Dominican preaching.[21] Other letters stressed Dominican pastoral care, through which Dominic tried, with the help of the papal letters and with reference to the Fourth Lateran Council, to make it clear to the bishops that they ought to regard the Dominicans as the "irreplaceable preachers" that canon 10 of the council had in mind. In this way he appealed to both the council and the authority of the Pope in support of Dominican preaching.[22] At the same time, the wrong use that certain Christians were making of the name *praedicator* was condemned in papal bulls. In a third group of letters supporting Dominic's plan, Dominican preaching was described as a "providential heavenly gift against heretics." This definition probably came from Pope Gregory IX rather than from Dominic himself.[23]

3. The Dominican Preaching Brothers' Understanding of
   Themselves

So far we have looked at the preaching of the Dominicans as
seen in papal documents. In 1220 the first general chapter of the
Dominicans was held in Bologna. At this chapter the factual
development of the order in the period following the Fourth
Lateran Council was codified. The order was seen as consisting
of preaching brethren who were authorized by papal authority
to proclaim the gospel without the restriction of diocesan boundaries and with exemption from the bishops.

As far as religious observances were concerned, the chapter
proceeded pragmatically, taking the constitutions of Prémontré
as their basic model, but elaborating these more flexibly in accord with Dominic's real concern, the free activity of preaching.
The brethren included all kinds of powers of dispensation in
favor of this free proclamation of the gospel, something completely new in religious legislation. The distinctively Dominican
aspect of this legislation can be seen above all in the formulation
of the aims of the Dominican Order and especially in the
chapters on the general chapter, on theological studies, and in
the definition of the "proclamation of the gospel."[24]

In the matter of proclaiming the gospel, emphasis was placed
in the general chapter on the apostolic lifestyle of the wandering
preachers. Despite the papal policy, which aimed to strengthen
the authority of the pope over the bishops via the new orders,
the Dominican Order was still very sensitive to the authority of
the local bishops. Exemption did not serve as an excuse for the
first Dominicans to cut across the traditional diocesan and
parish structures. In the light of Dominic's own experiences in
the south of France, they did, however, want "freedom to proclaim the gospel."[25] In this stance Dominic was inspired to a
great extent by the evangelical freedom of the early Waldensian
preachers, but, in contrast to them, he aimed at a symbiosis between Dominican preaching and the diocesan and parochial
structures.

These early constitutions make it clear that the Dominicans had to pay a visit to the local bishop when they first entered a diocese;[26] but despite this willingness to cooperate with the local clergy, it is also obvious from the constitutions that the *Ordo Praedicatorum* did not receive its mission to proclaim the gospel from the local bishops, but received it as an order approved by the pope. That is why the order itself, again and again in its general chapters, had to verify which of its individual members were competent to proclaim the gospel.[27] This free brotherhood of Christians, who were at the same time priests, regarding itself as an independent group of preachers — independent, that is, of the local episcopate — was something quite new canonically. Within the order, the virtue, reliability, evangelical commitment, and preaching ability of the Dominican candidates were applied as norms in determining competence for preaching.

As far as theological studies are concerned, the Dominicans were the first in the history of the Church's religious life to introduce a "study law."[28] Theology was the first condition for Dominican preaching activity, and priority was given to the study of theology over all the other traditional monastic observances. The preaching activity of every apostolic Dominican unit had to be watched over by a study-escort. (The Waldenses had a similar arrangement.) The two principal conditions for the Dominican *Praedicatio Jesu Christi*, then, were theological competence and the *vita apostolica*, or evangelical lifestyle. The way in which that lifestyle was in fact organized reflected this twofold demand.

Despite the fact that historically it was completely new and distinctive, this Dominican view was nonetheless situated firmly within the Church's medieval and feudal understanding of itself in the thirteenth century. In other words, it was based on the conviction that the gospel could not be authentically proclaimed without a hierarchical mission, either papal or episcopal. What is distinctively Dominican within this medieval view of the Church is that the Dominican had that mission precisely as a member of the *Ordo Praedicatorum*, that is, as one of a body of specialized preachers approved by the pope.[29]

III. The Inter-Clerical Struggle for the Authority to Preach: The Secular Clergy and the Mendicants

In the eleventh and twelfth centuries, there was conflict between the older monastic orders and the new institutions of canons regular because of new circumstances in the Church and the world. In the same way, in the second half of the thirteenth century there was a struggle between the Dominican and the Franciscan movement on the one hand and the diocesan clergy on the other. The latter reacted bitterly to the new movement, partly because a great deal of their financial income was flowing into the new orders. Here we are concerned only with the polemics regarding the competence to preach.

In 1255, a theologian from the diocesan clergy launched an attack against the activity of the mendicant friars, who, he claimed, were undermining the traditional system of pastoral care in the Church. This theologian, William of Saint-Amour, was the spokesman for many who believed that the rights of the local clergy had been fundamentally infringed upon by the papal privileges granted to the Dominicans and the Franciscans.

In this dispute, two different views of the Church were in collision: on the one hand, a view of the Church based on the autonomy of the local churches and, on the other, a view of the Church based on the privilege and primacy of the pope. In fact, Rome was making use of the mendicants to add greater force to the Roman policy of papal primacy over the episcopacy of the whole world. What is more, the entire financial basis of the medieval Church, which was founded on prebends, was seriously undermined by the right of the mendicants to beg. Because of the attacks made by representatives of the diocesan clergy, the Dominicans and Franciscans were obliged to provide a more precise theological justification for their authority to proclaim

the gospel. A new theology of office was developed in the process.

William of Saint-Amour used *auctoritates* from the *Decretum Gratiani* and Pseudo-Dionysius as arguments against the
praxis of the mendicants. According to his view, the mendicants were false prophets who arrogantly and wrongly claimed
competence to preach. His point of departure was the mediation
of the Church or the necessary *missio canonica* to preach, and he
rejected in principle any charismatic mission from the people of
God on the basis of the evangelical way of life. It was from God
that only the bishops had an exclusive right to preach, and that
exclusive right was, under their supervision, shared by the
parochial clergy, who were seen as the successors of the seventy-
two disciples sent out by Jesus.

According to William, then, the organization of pastoral
care in the Middle Ages was a divine right that was also binding
on the pope. Priesthood was, as it were, identified with the concept of pastor, the position belonging to the parochial clergy.
The Dominicans and Franciscans were seen anachronistically as
monks in the old style, and according to the law of the Church,
monks had no authority to preach. In their resistance to the
mendicants, then, the secular clergy identified the Church's office with territorially organized office. The Church was, in their
view, a kind of federation of diocesan and parochial local
churches, and even the pope himself was tied to this structure.
As a result, it was considered wrong for the pope to grant
privileges to extra-diocesan and extra-parochial clergy.

It is clear, therefore, that in this view the principle of the
essential bond between "community" and "office" that had prevailed in the early Church was narrowed down and territorially
confined. It also reflects a clear resistance on the part of the
diocesan clergy to the centralizing influences of the Curia. At the
same time, those who held this view increasingly stressed small
Church units as autarkic subjects, tracing these back to divine
right. They saw preaching as the monopoly of leaders of Chris-

tian communities and firmly rejected the principle of a supra-diocesan, specialized body of preachers.

They provided a theological justification for their teaching by appealing to the Pseudo-Dionysian doctrine of the hierarchy, which provided an ontological basis for it. According to this hierarchical thinking, which was seen as both heavenly and earthly, every efficient activity proceeded from above to below, and those who thought in this way refused to admit that any Church activity had a basis in the Church itself. The basis for any competence to preach was, in their opinion, not ordination, but *electio* or *missio canonica*. The new theology of the twelfth century, according to which the power to proclaim the gospel had a sacramental basis, was therefore once again abandoned and the power to preach was based on jurisdiction.

The tactical error of the mendicants was that they adopted the same jurisdictional standpoint. They did not have recourse to the experience of their own charism in their reply, when they could have defended it with an appeal to the *Statuta Ecclesiae antiqua*. In an attempt to defend their right to preach, they made a distinction between papal jurisdiction, which applied to the whole Church, and the bishops' jurisdiction, which was binding locally. They were victorious in the end, and the writings of William of Saint-Amour were eventually condemned by the pope. Because they had adopted the point of departure of those who opposed them, however, the medieval principle of the bond between *praedicatio* and *praelatio*, or the function of leadership, was perpetuated in the Church, with the result that lay people became the dupes of polemics among the clergy.

Thomas Aquinas had objections to this rigid hierarchical thinking, insisting that those who were of lower rank in the hierarchy could certainly teach those whose status was higher. In maintaining this position he was clearly opening the way, at least in principle, to the possibility of lay preaching, but he did not himself draw any conclusions of this kind. From the historical point of view, what was at stake at the time was not the theological possibility of lay preaching, but the emancipation of the clerical competence to preach from the traditional structures of pastoral care, those of the diocese and the parish.

The positive result that emerged from these polemics was that the proclamation of the Word of God could once again be seen as a qualified and specialized ministry within the whole complex of ministries required for the building up of a Christian community. Preaching did not in itself have to be connected with the leadership of a territorially organized community. The proclamation of the gospel was once again dissociated from its twelfth-century ontological basis and functionalized.

At the same time, the thirteenth-century theologians did not take into consideration the possibility that preaching could be based as well on the charisma of an evangelical life, with the result that they let a historical opportunity pass. This is particularly true of the Franciscans, who had begun as a lay movement but very soon became clericalized. The mendicants did not, in other words, break the bond between *praedicatio* and *praelatio*. What was ultimately at stake was the authority of the pope on the one hand and that of the bishops on the other. The fundamental question at issue, the proclamation of the gospel, was not really discussed.

IV. Is Lay Preaching Theologically Impossible?

According to the law of the Church currently in force, lay preaching is forbidden. Whether or not this has to do with the essential being of the Church itself is quite another question. It is clear that the prohibition against lay preaching had quite different origins and reasons in the history of the Church; it was connected with historical delineations of the authority of the one who had been placed in a position of leadership in the Church. From the historical point of view, it was a question of defending positions already achieved, and on a theological basis that defense was ideological. What is very paradoxical is that the thirteenth-century theology, which traces the whole question of proclaiming the Word of God back to jurisdiction, did, in principle at least, make lay preaching possible.

At the same time, however, Pope Gregory IX, in forbidding lay preaching, saw preaching as the exclusive right of the *ordo clericorum*.[30] Even now, in the twentieth century, there are bishops who claim that proclamation by a priest is "qualitatively different" from that by a lay person! The mysterious entity on which they base this assertion is puzzling. In fact, the theological competence of the lay person to speak in the midst of a community of brothers and sisters with the substantial authority of the gospel was never discussed in the medieval disputes about the right to preach. Other questions and other interests were at stake.

Canons from the *Statuta Ecclesiae antiqua*, dating from the second half of the fifth century and originating in South Gaul, were included in the *Decretum Gratiani*.[31] The key statement is: "Laicus autem praesentibus clericis, nisi ipsis rogantibus, docere non audeat": "Laymen may only preach in the presence of the clergy with their consent." This position had already been taken at an earlier period of the Church's history by Origen and Jerome.

According to the classical view on this issue, the basis for all proclamation in the Church is "being sent by Christ." From Jesus the mission to preach is given to the apostles and bishops, priests and deacons. This interpretation can, however, be explained in various ways. The concept "mission" is usually understood in a purely juridical sense, and what is at stake, then, is an institutional view of authority or competence. This juridical view, however, goes back to a period when there was an almost excessive supply of candidates, which meant that it was important to clarify who was permitted to proclaim the message of Jesus Christ in the name of the Church.

Our present problem, however, is not who is *permitted* to pass on the gospel message, but rather who *can* pass it on. Even the finest ecclesiological justifications cannot compensate for the fact that the Church's office does not at present bear up the one who proclaims the message. The very reverse is true. The individual who proclaims the Word of God has to confer a distinctive status on the Church's office by his or her personal commitment and his or her personal and social competence. Much more is contained in the biblical concept of "mission" than is included in the narrower juridical interpretation of the word.

According to the New Testament, mission is a task that is linked to the matter of Jesus. Jesus' message is passed on only where his life-praxis is followed. What, after all, made the Jews say: "He speaks as one who has authority and not as the scribes" (Matt 7:29)? The answer to this question is quite clear. Jesus made what he spoke about a direct and practical reality in the way he turned toward others. He did not, for example, say to Zacchaeus, "God loves you," as some fundamentalists do. On the contrary, he went home with him and by his praxis made God's love for Zacchaeus a living reality. Jesus' message was integrated into his active association with others to such a degree that his proclamation of the message and his praxis interpret each other and together change the concrete situation.

The approach of the kingdom of God was the central theme of Jesus' proclamation, and to such an extent that he gave it direct and free scope in and through his activity. In turning to the woman taken in adultery, to tax collectors and sinners, to children, to the sick, to cripples, and to the poor and oppressed, he made what he was speaking about directly visible and in this way anticipated the fulfillment of the kingdom of God. His proclamation affirmed the reality of God as salvation of and for all people in and through the accomplishment of his human existence as communicative praxis.

It is precisely this connection between Jesus' proclamation of his message and his living praxis that gives a very distinctive aspect to his way of speaking. He preached in the form of parables, stories involving translucent situations in which God's unconditional goodness revealed new possibilities to men and women: "So it is with the kingdom of God." The definition of the reality of God is closely connected with a particular form of communicative praxis. It takes place *in* action directed toward others. By his very existence and in his action, Jesus affirmed God as the saving reality. It was precisely because he persisted radically and uncompromisingly in turning toward human beings that he went toward death and accepted that death as the extreme price for the truth of his message.

The sending out of the disciples by Jesus was therefore not interpreted by New Testament Christians purely and simply as a mission to proclaim the Word of God, but also as an obligation to follow and imitate Jesus in an all-embracing *sequela Jesu,* an obligation to imitate his life-praxis by turning toward the people around them. This is clear from the most authentic words of Jesus used in the gospel in connection with the sending of his disciples: "He called to him his twelve disciples and gave them authority over unclean spirits . . . and to heal every disease and infirmity. . . . Go . . . and preach as you go, saying, 'The kingdom of heaven is at hand'" (Matt 10:1, 5, 7).

What emerges clearly from this and other texts is that the competence to proclaim the gospel is only part of a more complete, all-embracing reality, expressed in Jesus' life and praxis and ratified in his death. That reality is his turning toward those around him, the foundation of which was the "compassion" he had on the crowds (Matt 9:36). Like Jesus himself, his first disciples were men who originally led a wandering existence as missionaries in Palestine and who were bound to the guidelines given to them by Jesus. They took no money, no staff, no spare clothes with them (Matt 10:8-11). The post-paschal missionary Church used this mode of life to justify the conditions for a credible form of preaching. Like Jesus himself, the missionary Church had to adopt the same position from which Jesus preached, that is, the position of a wandering stranger, a guest who is at home nowhere and who is dependent on the hospitality of others — in other words, a position of impotence. The impression of power that proceeded from Jesus is intimately connected with this mode of presence.

The foundation of a Spirit-filled proclamation of the gospel "with power" is, therefore, faithfulness to the life-praxis of Jesus himself, the *sequela Jesu*. The mission to preach the message is justified insofar as, and on condition that, the proclamation is both a part and an expression of the imitation of Jesus. Imitation of Jesus as an inner aspect of that mission and as the obvious basis for the justification of the preacher is, moreover, valid not only in the initial period of community formation; it is constitutive also in the later phases, when there is always a danger that the institutional competence to preach will be overestimated.

Throughout the Church's history, there has always been a charismatic countermovement which, in the light of the evangelical *vita apostolica*, has called for the right to preach over and against the prescriptions of canonical conditions for admission to the preaching office. A purely juridical and institutional competence can quickly change into a competence that is adapted to "the Establishment," and this situation can often distort the gospel.

In view of the fact that a purely juridical mission can no longer serve as a justification for the proclamation of the message, there is a danger at present that the authentic basis will not be sought in the *vita apostolica*, the evangelical way of life, but rather in a more and more intensive theological specialization and in training programs for establishing communicative relationships. There is no doubt that these forms of specialized training have played an important part in the past twenty or so years in making preaching much more credible and effective. Nonetheless, professional catechists in every sector find themselves in a state of crisis.

Adapting the competence to preach the gospel to the norms and demands of socially comparable groups will not be sufficient for an evangelically credible form of preaching. The real norm and justification for competent proclamation of the gospel message is the praxis of Jesus himself embodied in the life of the preacher. The Christian who is really competent to preach today is one who, in his or her faith, is able to enter into the *sequela Jesu* fully. The competent preacher is one who can be totally concerned with human situations, one who can set in motion the processes of admiration, joy, and liberation that Jesus himself set in motion and continues to initiate today.

In that sense, bearing witness to faith and proclaiming the Christian message can never be a completely autonomous event. We are always overtaken by that to which we bear witness, and it comes upon us as grace. The foundation of all our proclamation is therefore an experience in which God takes the initiative. It is also always a fragment of Christian biography. That is why Francis of Assisi refused to accept the power to preach as a privilege granted by the pope. The evangelical power to preach was, in his view, to be found in the evangelical way of life. Dominic thought the same, but he also insisted from the very beginning that a sound theological training should be the second condition, protecting that evangelical witness from possible fanaticism and one sidedness.

Translated by David Smith

NOTES

1. J. P. Migne, ed., *Patrologia Latina* (henceforth *PL*), 221 vols. (Paris, 1844–64) 77:13-128.

2. E. Friedberg, ed., *Corpus iuris canonici* (Leipzig, 1879–81; reprint, Graz, 1959) 1:764.

3. *Ibid.*, 765.

4. *PL* 170:533-534.

5. See J. D. Mansi, *Sacrorum Conciliorum nova et amplissima collectio*, 31 vols. (reprint, Graz, 1960) 22:785.

6. M.-H. Laurent, ed., *Fabio Vigili et les bibliothèques de Bologne au début du XVI siècle*, Studi e testi 105 (Vatican City, 1948) no. 60.

7. *PL* 125:1356.

8. M.-H. Vicaire, *Histoire de saint Dominique*, 2 vols. (Paris, 1957) 1:229.

9. *Ibid.*

10. See *Conciliorum oecumenicorum decreta* (Bologna-Freiburg, 1962) 215.

11. P. Mandonnet, *Saint Dominique: L'Idée, l'homme, et l'oeuvre*, 2 vols. (Paris, 1957) 1:229.

12. *Conciliorum oecumenicorum decreta* 218.

13. H. Grundmann, *Religiöse Bewegungen im Mittelalter*, 2nd ed. (Hildesheim, 1961) 141–142.

14. *Ibid.*, 142–152.

15. See Friedberg, 1:1097–1098.

16. See Vicaire, 2:48–51; H. C. Scheeben, *Der heilige Dominikus* (Freiburg im Breisgau, 1927) 95, 125.

17. See Vicaire, 2:55–61, 65–74.

18. Laurent, no. 84.

19. See Vicaire, 2:76–77; 279–290.

20. Laurent, no. 87; Vicaire, 2:82, 88.

21. Laurent, no. 103.

22. See Vicaire, 2:289.

23. *Ibid.*, 250; Laurent, nos. 112, 127.

24. See A. H. Thomas, *Die Oudst Constituties van de Dominicanen* (Louvain, 1965); Vicaire, 2:157ff.; Mandonnet, 2:273–292.

25. Vicaire, 2:166.

26. Mandonnet, 2:291.

27. *Ibid.*, 288; Vicaire, 2:157.

28. Mandonnet, 2:290.

29. Vicaire, 2:54.

30. Friedberg, 2:789.

31. See *Decretum Gratiani* 23, 29; Friedberg, 1:86; C. Munier, *Les Statuta Ecclesiae Antiqua* (Paris, 1957) 137.

A *Response* by Maureen P. Carroll, O.P.

As a catalyst to the fourth stated purpose of this symposium: "To lay a theological foundation for the expansion of the notion of preaching by the faithful," I will situate my two points of response within Schillebeeckx's own theological project in a somewhat broader way than is first indicated by this essay. My remarks will deal: (1) with his critical method of interpreting the past; and (2) with his foundation in experience for the right to preach in the notion of *vita apostolica.*

I. *Schillebeeckx's Method of Interpreting Texts and Events of the Past*

The interpretative character of this essay is pronounced from the outset. With detailed scholarship, Schillebeeckx places magisterial statements concerning lay preaching and the current practice of restricting it into their historical contexts. He affirms that this hermeneutical task is essential to our theological reflection on preaching by lay persons in the present situation of the Church. Thus, what may appear to be a mere historical review of generally available developments becomes, rather, a process of interpretation, leading to his unmistakable conclusion that *there is no theological basis for the exclusion of non-ordained Christians with suitable credentials from the ministry of preaching in the Church.* In fact, the question of preaching by non-ordained persons as such was not even raised in a serious theological way at the time of the prohibition of their exercising this ministry. Special interest groups, in their desire to retain power and to prevent others from acquiring it, and in their hierarchical conceptions of the relationships between men and women in the order of creation and between cleric and lay in the ecclesiastical order, prevented the question from receiving a hearing in any real theological sense. This much is certainly clear from Schillebeeckx's essay, though his historical interpretation of relevant events and texts will continue to be debated and re-worked by others.

What is it about his interpretative method that may prove useful to us? Schillebeeckx is conscious that the *past* is always read and understood in light of *present* questions and *present* situations. The question about the theological foundation for preaching in the Church by its non-ordained members is *our* question. It is a question born of our new experiences of ourselves as educated lay persons; as Christians with a consciousness of ministerial aptitudes in the plurality of ecclesial ministries; and as women or men who are often marginalized by the very structures that are meant to serve the proclamation of the gospel in which we believe. The very topic that sparked this conference would have been impossible to consider in most earlier contexts of Christian experience.

What is *not* at work in Schillebeeckx's method, then, is the application of answers and adaptations from the past to our situation. This is a doomed methodology, in his view, and is invalid in light of our own new situation, culturally and ecclesially. Certainly Schillebeeckx's hermeneutics values the past tremendously; but, typically, it looks to a *particular aspect* of the past – to an as yet unachieved aspect – for aid in interpreting our own dilemmas and in acting on our own questions. Thus, we find our deepest bond with the medievals, who, for a host of reasons, legislated against preaching by lay persons and against the liturgical involvement of women, not in their ideologies but in their evangelical hopes. In their efforts to reform evangelical preaching, they give oblique evidence of hoping for that which we, too, desire and which our children will desire after us: namely, *the coming of the reign of God promised by Jesus of Nazareth and the mandate to remove impediments to its arrival.*

This *productive* memory of the past – a constant theme in Schillebeeckx's work on tradition – is unfortunately less emphasized in this essay than it might have been, though, in fact, its whole structure is a productive historical interpretation. This remembering of the past is oriented toward the future and is thus suggestive of actions we must take in the present. Elsewhere he remarks that "critical remembrances of events in the past have a power to open up the future" (*Ministry*, p. 3). Surely his concluding words about the preaching and praxis of Jesus as the announcement of the coming reign of God are illustrative of my point that his "historical review" of medieval developments is intrinsically directed toward achieving the future we share with them.

But this is also a *critical* memory of the past. Schillebeeckx traces a number of the ideological and repressive elements of the ecclesial past that have contributed to the present ministerial order. Here, too, he is less explicit than he has been in other recent works — *Jesus*, *Christ*, and *Ministry*, in particular. For example, the helpful concept of the *contrast experience*, so crucial to his theology of historical experience, would have been useful here in describing and interpreting more fully the productive nature of the painful experiences of lay persons who belie the unschooled, worldly caricature of earlier ecclesiastical portraits, or of women whose talents and training for preaching the gospel publicly far outrun the present canonical legislation concerning the authorized ministries available to them. A new situation has come into existence in the Church. A contrast is often experienced between what one hopes to be — indeed, what one is apparently called by God to be, by reason of natural and acquired gifts for ministry — and yet what one is forbidden by present ecclesial discipline from being and doing.

In this painful contrast, Schillebeeckx elsewhere notes, a cognitive *diagnosis* is made of the present, unhealthy situation; a *criticism* is offered of the decisions and the structures that keep this situation in force; and a *dynamism* is unleashed to produce alternate forms of ministry (*Ministry*, pp. 79–80). This threefold cognitive-critical-productive configuration is the same as that which Schillebeeckx accords the occurrence of divine revelation within our human experiences, for there is genuine authority that emanates from an experience of critical yet hopeful contrast. A call to the hidden meaning of Christian conversion is lodged in this very sort of experience. For the present, however, the proclamation of the gospel is hindered. Non-ordained and ordained members of the community are forced to confront elements of their experience that threaten the building up of the *ecclesia*—elements that alienate where they were once meant to unite, and that subvert rather than illuminate the meaning of the text "Go and preach the gospel to all nations." Schillebeeckx is quick to note that the alternative praxis that will have to be taken up by some—"on the grounds of the right of the Christian community to become a true community of Jesus and to extend that community"—must be prepared "to be seen through the medium of what is bound to be regarded as at least temporarily illegal," as, indeed, has always been the case in the Church ("The Christian Community and Its Office Bearers," *Concilium* 133, pp. 121–122).

All this, together with necessary cautions, is made explicit in a wide range of Schillebeeckx's theological ventures. His hermeneutics regards *current experiences* as essential to our grasp of what the gospel itself means, has always meant, and will continue to mean for ongoing history. His purpose in this essay evidently did not extend to the analysis of the present experiences of lay persons who do preach in the Church and of those who hear them; nor to the negative experiences of those believers who are qualified by appropriate theological expertise, recognized by their respective communities as leaders and/or prophets, and desirous of a public ministry of proclaiming the gospel, yet are prevented from doing so by historical and not properly theological elements in their Church's tradition. In light of the changed historical situation in which we find ourselves, I would suggest that this analysis and theological reflection in the interests of possible alternate forms of praxis are ingredient to the work of this conference and are impelled by Schillebeeckx's own interpretative method.

II. *"Vita Apostolica" as the Foundation in Experience for the
   Ministry of Preaching*

Let us first ask: How does this concept function in establishing the basis for a believer's right to preach and for a community's right to ask for the preachers it needs? *Vita apostolica,*
a term whose content and meaning are perhaps much less obvious than we might initially suppose, is a critical and productive tool for Schillebeeckx.

First, it is a *critical* concept. The New Testament's notion of
the "apostolic life" is explicitly based on the lifestyle of Jesus of
Nazareth and has been embraced historically, with numerous
cultural variations, by all true disciples of the Lord. What the
concept *vita apostolica* always does for us is to recall our under-
standings of effective ministry to the saving, healing, teaching
ministry of Jesus himself and to the apparent failure of that prophetic ministry. Witness the way in which Schillebeeckx
employs the notion to criticize the deficiencies of any "slick pro-
fessionalism" or sheer "performance-oriented" homiletics training today. The concept sharpens the edge of the requisite aca-
demic and professional preparation for preaching by constantly
measuring it against Jesus' own evangelical charisms.

Secondly, it is a *productive* concept. We must interpret the
meaning of *vita apostolica* by incorporating: (1) not only the
foundational testimony of the Scriptures and Christian tradition
to Jesus and to the various ways in which men and women have
embarked upon the *imitatio Iesu Christi* in the past; (2) but also,
and just as essentially, our own experiences of attempting to live
and articulate the gospel we have heard, as people living in this
world, in this society, in this Church.

What are the practical and theoretical contours of *vita
apostolica* for ourselves? What I am suggesting — as I believe
Schillebeeckx also to be implying — is that there are aspects of
the apostolic way of life that are only now coming to light
because of our own efforts to be Christian believers in this new
social and ecclesial context. This will always be the case, in fact.

As with the gospel itself, so the gospel way of life is by no means a fully evident reality in the world or in the Church as yet. It is finally an eschatological notion, partaking of the reign of God that is yet to come.

I believe that two qualifications can prove helpful to our understanding of what Schillebeeckx means by placing *vita apostolica* at the very foundation of the right and the authority to preach. First, the notion of *vita apostolica* is markedly *experiential*. We must be careful not to make of it an ideal, and then to identify this ideal with particular forms of apostolic living that arose in other historical contexts — at least, not to do this in an uncritical, unconscious way. For example, there is need for salutary caution against identifying *vita apostolica* prematurely with celibate life as it has evolved in religious communities of women and men, with spiritualist revival movements, with liturgical renewal groups, or with service-oriented social agencies. Rather, the question we want to ask is: Have we yet sufficiently explored the dimensions of our own experiences and those of our contemporaries to say with surety what are the requirements of apostolic commitment in the style of Jesus of Nazareth in *this* globally and cosmically conscious world, confronted with the specter of nuclear dissolution at its own hands? What are the political and social exigencies of the apostolic life today? For Schillebeeckx, this issue forms the very soul of his current "Jesus" project. And, for ourselves, this question lies at the foundation of our considerations of who has the right to preach in the Church today.

Secondly, the notion of *vita apostolica* is also *practical*, as is Schillebeeckx's foundation for the right to preach. His theology of preaching rests on what he here terms the "communicative praxis" of Jesus on behalf of human salvation and liberation. Only derivatively is it a theology of the Word as such. The preached Word puts a "name" to the import of the *action* taken on behalf of the freedom of others. The preached Word, which summons the believer to such action, is also meant to make it clear that the praxis of human liberation is grounded in the universal saving action of our God in history. Jesus' words were able to move his hearers to expect in joy the coming of God's reign because his actions afforded them an experience in their own lives of the onset of that reign.

In view of this practical definition of *vita apostolica* as the foundation for the Christian disciple's preaching ministry, the question before us must constantly be: What kind of "communicative praxis" — both within the community of believers and outside of it — will serve to anticipate the justice and peace of the reign of God, and not function as a countersign to Christian hope among believers and non-believers alike? The pastoral intention of Schillebeeckx's theology raises this issue repeatedly. Can we ignore today the urgent pastoral problem of the disaffection of many believers — those who suffer from the racial, sexual, economic, or even cultic prejudices of the larger community — who are estranged from the worshipping Church and the proclamation of its gospel because they cannot hear a message of liberation for themselves in its official teachings? What praxis of reconciliation is first called for within the community itself as the authentication of all our apostolic preaching? Schillebeeckx elsewhere refers to a type of Christian "obedience" to the authority of those who suffer unjustly in the human community. What disobedience to, or dissent from, oppressive pieces of legislation might be exacted of preachers and theologians who seek to announce to these new "little ones" in our midst: "The reign of God has come upon you"? I would suggest that this is, at least, a fair question for us to consider.

I maintain, then, that Schillebeeckx has offered us valuable practical and theoretical tools. I have mentioned: (1) his critical method of understanding the present situation regarding lay preaching, in view of the past of Christian tradition and the future of Christian expectation; and (2) his employing the critical notion of *vita apostolica* as the foundation in experience for the right to preach and to call others to preach in the community. I might have mentioned other extremely useful critical tools—in particular, the charismatic nature of countermovements in the Church, according to Schillebeeckx's theology of the Holy Spirit's activity in human history. But it is futile to attempt to mine all the resources that his theology-with-a-pastoral-intent provides for a group such as this.

WORKS OF SCHILLEBEECKX CITED:

Christ. The Experience of the Lord. Trans. John Bowden. New York: The Seabury Press, 1980.

Jesus. An Experiment in Christology. Trans. Hubert Hoskins. New York: The Seabury Press, 1979.

Ministry. Leadership in the Community of Jesus Christ. Trans. John Bowden. New York: The Seabury Press, 1981.

A *Response* by Donald Goergen, O.P.

I want to emphasize three points in Father Schillebeeckx's paper: (1) He is implicitly suggesting the value to the Church of pluralism within the preaching office. The Church need not limit itself to one model. There is room and need in the Church for the preaching of the pope, of the bishops, of the priests, as well as for supra-parochial and supra-diocesan preachers, for preaching by monks and by the laity, for preaching by women and by men. The trend in the Middle Ages to narrow and restrict the preaching office can be reversed.

(2) If we raise the question of who has the right to preach, or what criteria we can use for preaching in the name of the Church, there are at least three criteria to which Schillebeeckx refers at various places. In fact, all three of these criteria he sees within the Dominican preaching movement; all three were present in the formulation of the first general chapter at Bologna in 1220. These are (a) evangelical life, or the *vita apostolica;* (b) theological competence and training; and (c) preaching in cooperation with the local bishop.

Schillebeeckx gives a primacy, of course, to the first of these — *vita apostolica.* It is this evangelical life, which is an imitation of the life praxis of Jesus, that authorizes anyone to preach, whether ordained or non-ordained. Yet, the second criterion — theological competence — is also important; it follows after the conversion to the life praxis of Jesus, but it is reflected in the Dominican "study law." One ought not preach who has not studied in order to do so. The third criterion — preaching in cooperation with the local bishop — Schillebeeckx mentions less explicitly, except to note how Dominican friars were to visit the bishop of a diocese before preaching there — not that they received their authorization to preach from the bishop, but that their preaching might be with the Church rather than against the Church. It is the first of these, however, that Schillebeeckx calls most strongly to our attention.

(3) Finally, I want to point to the connection Schillebeeckx draws between a theology of preaching and Christology. Questions connected with the preaching office are not only ecclesiological but also christological. Who is Jesus? We preach Christ crucified and raised from the dead. In Mark 1:38, Jesus identifies his own mission with that of preaching; yet he preaches by word *and* deed. His life praxis proclaims the reign of God. The symbolic language of the parables is consistent with the symbolic actions of his life. Jesus goes to the house of Zacchaeus, shares fellowship at table with outcasts and sinners, washes the feet of his disciples. Mission there is not only an ecclesiastical/jurisdictional question; it is a theological/christological question. Jesus himself was someone so grasped by the reign of God that he could do no other than proclaim it; so likewise is the preacher.

A *Response* by Mary Catherine Hilkert, O.P.

My reflections center around Schillebeeckx's understanding of tradition and fidelity to the living tradition which is the Church. That understanding, which provides one key to Schillebeeckx's larger theological project, is an important underlying theme in the paper we have just heard—a theme that has very real implications for this conference.

In his discussion of the history of lay preaching and its prohibition, Schillebeeckx continually highlights moments of change when something *new* was introduced into the tradition, usually on the basis of some "contrast experience"—some experience of conflict during a time when the impulse of the Spirit was active in the Church calling forth a new response to the gospel. As Schillebeeckx has noted elsewhere, fidelity to a living tradition is to be found not in doing today what has always been done in the past, but rather in responding in a new and creative way to the same gospel mandate (in this case, the preaching of the gospel to the ends of the earth) in our own historical moment and in the new and different cultural experiences in which we find ourselves.

Such a living fidelity involves both a "critical remembering" of our history and an openness to perceive what God's Spirit is saying in our own new moment in the tradition. For Schillebeeckx, the process of a critical retrieval of the tradition involves looking for unnoticed and forgotten persons or moments in the past and asking how far the history of the past contains a future dimension that we have not yet seriously taken account of, while at the same time identifying distortions that have been operative in the living tradition.

Schillebeeckx has analyzed distortion in our tradition primarily in terms of the clericalization of the preaching ministry and power struggles among the clergy. Another distortion that he alluded to at one point but did not develop in this paper is the domination structure of sexism—a real factor in our tradition that has distorted our perception of who is called to preach in the Christian community. Following Schillebeeckx's lead in further work along this line, we might take another look even at Thomas Aquinas and a forgotten section of the *Summa Theologiae* in which he discusses whether women are endowed with the charism of speaking words of wisdom and knowledge in the Christian community (II-II, q. 177, a.2). There Aquinas clearly grants that women are gifted with this charism. He even gives examples of such forgotten women in our history, but his limited anthropology and his view that women are necessarily subject to men in the "natural hierarchy" led him to the conclusion that women should exercise this charism in private. Using Schillebeeckx's method of interpreting a living tradition, we could retrieve what has gone unnoticed in Aquinas's writings while remaining critical of the domination structures that kept him from arriving at the conclusion that women could preach publicly in the Christian community.

As is perhaps even more evident in some of Schillebeeckx's other recent writings than in the paper presented here, his approach to a contemporary question such as preaching by the non-ordained in relation to the tradition of the Church would not be one of simply searching history for evidence in the past of lay preaching or women preaching — although he has conducted that search in this paper and found evidence of both. Even more significantly, however, his method of interpretation would ask: "What is our situation now? What call is God speaking precisely in and through our human experience and our experience of Church?" Those very experiences, and especially experiences that contrast with what the Church community *should* be, are revelatory of the Holy Spirit active in the Church today.

In light of that understanding of tradition as an ongoing history of lived experience, a real part of our theological work these days should include reflection on our own experience, including our experiences of contrast and conflict:

— our experience of preaching as non-ordained persons;

— our experience of hearing the Word proclaimed by women, by married persons, by single persons who are not ordained;

— our experience of the preaching of the Church when it is totally limited to the experience of the clerical, male, and predominantly celibate members of the community;

— our experience of bishops and local churches that *do* call forth and encourage lay preaching in the Church today;

— our experience of being prohibited from preaching or unable to call forth the preachers we felt could best speak the Word in our midst at a particular celebration.

In other words, we need to reflect on our experience of our own times and the various cultural situations and local churches in which we find ourselves in order to hear what the Spirit is saying in the living tradition of the Church today. What faithful response to the Church's constant mandate to preach the gospel is being called for in these *new* times?

My second set of observations comes in response to Schillebeeckx's comments about the "tactical errors" made in medieval times and the importance of the "point of departure" in any discussion of lay preaching. How we frame our discussions and which questions we ask are very important decisions. The very structure and topics of this conference suggest new starting points for the discussion of preaching by the non-ordained. They move the question from that of when the jurisdiction to preach can be extended to lay persons to that of a deeper consideration of charisms and ministries within the Christian community.

Here we need to note that we are talking about the charisms of baptized persons and not necessarily of those who are members of a religious congregation or order that has as its mission the preaching of the gospel. It is important, too, that we not limit our understanding of preaching to liturgical preaching, although that is a major issue we are addressing here, but rather that we see the interconnectedness of all the Church's preaching with the celebration of Eucharist. Then our discussions will become not a question of "Can lay persons preach?" but reflection on the experience of lay preaching that is, in fact, going on in many ways in our various church communities. It is in light of that broader community experience that we then need to raise the question regarding roles in the liturgical assembly, and specifically, "Who should proclaim the Word in that context?"

Further, in framing our discussions, let us not forget the topic that was originally publicized as the title of Professor Schillebeeckx's presentation this evening: "The Right of the Christian Community to a Preacher." Schillebeeckx has written elsewhere that a common starting point for discussions about Church ministries should be that of the Christian community's right to do everything necessary to become a true community of Jesus and to extend that community. Obviously those rights would include the right of the community to hear the Word of God proclaimed.

With that in mind, we need to ask in specific pastoral situations: Who can best enflesh and proclaim the Word of God here and now — in this racial group, for these women, for this group of children, etc.? What will most ensure their right and provide for their need to hear the Word of God in a way that speaks to their experience? As Professor Schillebeeckx has written in this paper, it is not a question of who is permitted to preach, but of who *can* preach? Who can best mediate the Word of God in this community situation?

Finally, I would suggest that we need to continue to raise questions about authorization in preaching. There is a valid concern that preaching be done in the name of the Church and that it be the gospel of Jesus Christ that is proclaimed. For that reason we need to keep returning to the question of how we discern and test charisms in the Christian community. What other models of community discernment are possible? On both a theological and pastoral level, then, what is the relationship between the two authorities that Schillebeeckx describes in his paper — the bishops of the Church in their very real role of leadership and responsibility within the Christian community, and the charismatic authority of those called by grace and a gospel life to proclaim the gospel in public in the midst of their brothers and sisters?

A *Response* by William Skudlarek, O.S.B.

About ten years ago I was writing a doctoral dissertation on lay preaching in the high Middle Ages and had to work my way through many of the same sources that Father Schillebeeckx drew upon for his presentation. I thought it was because of my dissertation that I had been invited to be a respondent this evening. However, after reading and listening to Father Schillebeeckx's paper, I began to wonder if I were not being called upon to make amends for all those medieval monks who sold out to the canons by making their priesthood the basis for their right to preach!

As one who has spent considerable time sifting through the medieval sources that deal with lay preaching, I am especially grateful to Father Schillebeeckx for the masterful way in which he has gathered and interpreted these materials. In my response I would like to call attention to some additional materials from the medieval period that I believe can also be helpful to the contemporary discussion of lay preaching in the Church.

My study of lay preaching in the high Middle Ages focused on the response of Pope Innocent III to the lay preaching movements of his day, especially the Waldenses and the Franciscans. One of my principal findings was that while Pope Innocent agreed with the Catholic theologians of the day who insisted that lay preaching could not be justified simply by holiness of life (the *vita apostolica*) and needed ecclesial authorization, he was careful not to make this ecclesial authorization the basis of the right to preach. That right was rooted in a divine mission, or, as we would say today, in charism.

Pope Innocent understood the ecclesial mission as a confirmation of the divine mission, a way of commissioning those preachers whom the Lord had raised up and called to spread his word. Evidence for this interpretation of Pope Innocent's view can be found in a letter dating from the year 1206 which the Pope wrote to the hierarchy of Poland, asking them to support the abbot of Langheim in his missionary endeavors among the pagans (*PL* 215:1010f.). In this letter Pope Innocent interprets the *locus classicus* of Rom 10:15 ("How can they preach unless they are sent?") in such a way that the ecclesial sending is seen to follow upon the action of God on the individual: God calls a person to preach, and this person in turn goes to the Lord's vicar on earth (so it was that Innocent understood his office) to be sent by him into the harvest.

I would suggest that Pope Innocent interpreted the ecclesial authorization of the preacher as a quasi-sacramental sign of the divine call. For Innocent, the whole of humanity is the Lord's field. Those who hold office in the Church are laborers whom the Lord, in his absence, has entrusted with the work of bringing in the harvest. This harvest belongs to the Lord, but since he has returned to his Father (that is, since he is no longer visibly present), the work of gathering the produce must be left to his visible representatives.

This interpretation of Pope Innocent's understanding of the need for a visible mission, a public licensing of one who is called to the office of preaching, is aided by the fact that he begins his letter with a clear reference to the first chapter of the Epistle to the Romans and Paul's argument against those who would excuse the sins of the pagans on the grounds that they had received no special revelation of the existence and will of God. The invisible God, Paul says, has made it possible for people to know him through his visible works. Innocent carries the argument one step further by pointing to Jesus as the culminating and most obvious of these visible works. That is, in fact, the very meaning of Jesus Christ: he is the visibility, the historical presence of the Father. Hence, Innocent argues, those who would engage themselves in the preaching of Jesus Christ must themselves be marked by some visible sign of commissioning, must be authorized in a public way by the Church, which continues to make visibly present the work of God in the world — which is the work of Jesus Christ.

If God had chosen to accomplish human salvation simply through an interior call, through the invisible working of the Spirit on human consciousness, then perhaps no such public mission would be needed. But the record of his deeds, above all, the fact of Jesus Christ, indicates that this is not the way he has chosen; he works rather through external signs, in the created order, and therefore an ecclesial mission is necessary for one who wishes to announce the gospel.

The fact that Innocent does not, however, isolate and exalt the ecclesial mission to the point of primary importance bears underlining. Given the critical situation of the times, it is a reaction one might be led to expect, especially from this "jurist pope." Hence, it is all the more striking that Innocent uses the text from Rom 10:15 ("How can they preach unless they are sent?"), a text that had constantly been thrown in the face of lay preachers to prove that they were not legitimate preachers, since they had received no ecclesial mission. Innocent interprets this text as referring at least indirectly to the call of God. His interpretation might seem a bit on the clever side, however, for he sees the divine call not simply in terms of a call to preaching, but as a call to preaching *and* to the seeking of papal approval for that preaching. Nonetheless, he does not do away with, or even reduce to a position of secondary importance, the divine initiative in the work of preaching the gospel. It is God who raises up preachers; the Church approves and deploys those so raised.

What I am suggesting here is that in the medieval sources on lay preaching, especially those relating to Pope Innocent III's involvement in the controversy, there are hints of an approach to the relationship between charism and office that are close to more contemporary attempts to describe this relationship, especially as these are to be found in modern theologies of baptism and orders. If I am correct in my reading of contemporary sacramental theology and ecclesiology, ordination is interpreted less and less in terms of the granting of power; it is seen rather as a way of "ordering" the power given to all Christians in virtue of their baptism. One of the most striking instances of such an interpretation is to be found in the Decree on the Church's Missionary Activity *(Ad Gentes)* of the Second Vatican Council. Addressing the question of the restoration of the permanent diaconate, the document reads:

> there are men who are actually carrying out the functions of the deacon's office, either by preaching the Word of God as catechists, or by presiding over scattered Christian communities in the name of the pastor and the bishop, or by practicing charity in social or relief work. It will be helpful to strengthen them by that imposition of hands which has come down from the apostles, and to bind them more closely to the altar. Thus they can carry out their ministry more effectively because of the sacramental grace of the diaconate (no. 16).

We see here a coming together of charism and order. The recommendation that the diaconate be restored as a permanent order in the Roman Catholic Church is based on the observation that the ministry is already being exercised, and that the charism thus manifested be formally recognized by the community, and strengthened by prayer and a closer relationship to worship. It could perhaps still be argued that this "formal recognition" confers a power that was not there before ordination, but obviously the emphasis here is not on the conferral of powers but on the recognition and "ordering" of gifts and on making explicit that these gifts of service are signs (sacraments) of the ministry of Christ in the Church.

Although Father Schillebeeckx could not be expected to treat all the issues surrounding lay preaching, I do confess to some disappointment over his failure to develop more fully the question of the relationship between preaching and the celebration of the sacraments. He alluded to this relationship in his reference to the Fourth Lateran Council, which recommended that

> in cathedral churches as well as in conventual churches suitable men be appointed whom the bishops may use as coadjutors and assistants, not only in the office of preaching but also in hearing confession, imposing penances, and in other matters that pertain to the salvation of souls (Canon X).

In other words, the preacher who calls people to conversion should also be able to offer the sacramental sign of the forgiveness of sins and reconciliation with the Father.

If there is a logical connection between the call to conversion and the celebration of the sacrament of reconciliation, that logical connection also extends to the proclamation of the Good News and the response of praise and thanksgiving (Eucharist) with which the Good News is received. Such a connection is to be found in the medieval sources on lay preaching. Not infrequently lay preachers celebrated the Eucharist. Catholic polemicists were quick to pounce on these illegitimate celebrations as proof that the preachers were arrogant anti-clericalists. However, such may not always have been the case. For example, Bernard Prim, the lay leader of a community known as the Poor Lombards, came to Rome in the spring of 1210 to seek papal approval for himself and his followers. In the *propositum vitae* they made on that occasion, they profess that they did not celebrate the Eucharist

> for reasons of presumption, or out of contempt for the sacrifice of the priest, but because of a burning faith and love, and after having decided that the simple faithful who lived among the heretics and had no occasion to receive the Eucharist, would become confirmed in their error (*PL* 216:291).

The link between preaching and the sacraments, especially the Eucharist, is a close one. We need to consider it carefully, not so much to limit who may preach, but to widen our understanding of who may rightfully lead a community in its sacramental response of praise and thanksgiving to a God who has revealed himself as a loving and gracious Father.

New Testament Foundations for Preaching by the Non-Ordained

SANDRA SCHNEIDERS, I.H.M.

The question of the bearing of New Testament material on the issue of preaching by the non-ordained is both very important and very complex. Unless we formulate the question itself with great precision, we risk a discussion that might be edifying, even illuminating, but, in the long run, useless in dealing with the urgent pastoral problem that gave rise to this colloquium, namely, the need to ground, biblically and theologically, the extension of the ministry of liturgical preaching to the non-ordained.

Consequently, in the first part of this paper I will attempt to clarify the question itself, as I understand it. Then I will discuss the question of methodology in the use of the New Testament material to deal with the question. Third, I will discuss the New Testament material that I consider most relevant to the question and most likely to foster the development of a fruitful response.

In the second part of the paper, I will "launch out into the deep," so to speak, in an attempt to lay some New Testament foundations for a more adequate theology of preaching than that which undergirds the current discipline.

I. The Historical Questions

A. *The Question*

As you are undoubtedly aware, canon 766 of the revised Code of Canon Law, promulgated by Pope John Paul II on January 25, 1983, does not exclude all preaching by lay people.

It excludes the unordained only from the preaching of the homily during the Eucharistic liturgy. In this respect, it is less stringent than its predecessor, canon 1342 of the former Code, which expressly forbade any preaching in the Church by lay persons, even religious.

Presumably, canon 766 of the revised Code will not cancel the exception, granted in 1973, allowing for a dialogue homily or for someone other than the ordained to give the homily in liturgies celebrated with children.[1] These details are important if we are to formulate the question honestly as well as precisely. If the non-ordained can, in some cases — for example in liturgies with children — legitimately preach, then there is no intrinsic reason, that is, no reason pertaining to the very essence of preaching or of its relationship to the Eucharistic liturgy, that requires that it be done by the ordained. We are dealing with a disciplinary arrangement, and we can legitimately inquire why this discipline is deemed necessary or desirable.

It may have been the case in times past, especially when few people were literate, much less trained in the sacred sciences, that the restriction of preaching to the ordained was both wise and necessary, since only those with a clerical education would be competent for this ministry. Today, especially in countries like our own, there are large numbers of non-ordained Catholics who are not only adequately trained in the sacred sciences but better trained than the average clergyman. Thus, the requirement of competence in the preacher is not the reason for the prevailing discipline. Since all males in the Church, whether celibate or married, are eligible for ordination, either to the presbyterate or to the diaconate, and all women in the Church are excluded from both, it is difficult to avoid the conclusion that the present legislation restricting liturgical preaching to the ordained is tantamount to excluding women from this ministry.

Our question, then, in the first part of this paper, is actually twofold: first, whether women should be excluded from liturgical preaching; second, whether liturgical preaching should

be restricted to the ordained, no matter who is eligible for ordination now or at any time in the future. Once we have re-
sponded to these preliminary questions, we will proceed to the
more important question, namely, what are the real biblical
foundations for the ministry of preaching and what does reflection on this material suggest to us as individuals and as an ecclesial community?

B. *Method*

Before dealing substantively with the questions before us, it
is necessary to raise the question of method. Obviously, the
New Testament, which does not tell us anything about ordination or about who presided or preached at Eucharistic liturgy,
does not provide a straightforward answer to our questions
about the exclusion of women from preaching or the restriction
of this ministry to the ordained. If the New Testament is to function at all in our inquiry, it must be in some less direct fashion.

Basically, there are two approaches to the text that one might
take in addressing questions of this type to the New Testament.
The first is what I might call historical fundamentalism. It attempts to find texts which, taken in isolation from their literary
and historical contexts, seem explicitly to answer the questions
raised or support answers already formulated. Thus, a literal appeal to the reference in 2 Tim 1:6 regarding Paul's laying hands
on Timothy would be adduced to prove that Paul ordained his
successors to the episcopacy.[2] Or a similar appeal to the text in 1
Cor 14:34-35 about women keeping silence in the churches
would be brought forward as a prohibition in perpetuity of any
oral liturgical participation by women. Needless to say, this fun-
damentalistic approach to the New Testament is, at best, scien-
tifically suspect.

The second approach is a historically responsible theological
interpretation of the data. The first task in such an approach is a
strictly historical one — the effort to find out what was actually
done and taught in the earliest Christian communities that might

have a bearing on our contemporary questions. We must raise questions about when and how Church order developed, what offices evolved in various communities and how the roles of the officeholders were understood, and how office was related to ministry.[3] We need to ask whether women were restricted from exercising certain ministries, and if so, why. Were such restrictions universal? Did they arise from theological or purely cultural considerations? And were the reasons then adduced for such restrictions valid either for their own time or for later ages? However, once we have unearthed all the historical data that the text, critically investigated within its cultural and literary context, can yield, we must go on to the much more difficult question of how to apply those data to the contemporary situation.

Here again scholarship is divided. There are those who would insist that the earliest Christian communities are a blueprint for the later Church.[4] Everything done in the New Testament period must, or at least can, be replicated today; nothing really new is legitimate. Not everyone who espouses this position is literalistic or reactionary. Much of the effort that has gone into showing, from the New Testament text, that women were called to apostleship by Jesus is motivated by the conviction that if this can be shown to be the case, the Church would no longer have an argument for excluding women from holy orders. This conviction is the counterpoint to the same approach used by Church officials who initiated the discussion by claiming that if Jesus did not call women to apostleship, the Church can never ordain women.[5]

In my opinion, this approach to the historical material in the New Testament is inadequate. The real question is not *whether* such or such a thing was done or not done by Jesus or the early Church but *why*. Only if we can establish that something was done or taught for sound theological reasons that continue to obtain today can a practice and teaching enshrined in the New Testament be considered normative for us. We are not called to slavish mimicry of first-century thought and practice, even that of Jesus, but to put on the mind of Christ, who, under the impulse of the Spirit and in obedience to his Father, gave himself up for us and incorporated us into his divine filiation and salvific mission so that we might extend God's love to the ends of the earth.

But, one might ask, what is the purpose of historical investigation of the New Testament data if one is not going to apply it literally and normatively to the present? In my opinion, the usefulness of the historical data, though limited, is quite real. First of all, it is the facts we uncover that orient us correctly to the significant questions that relate to our present concerns. Discovering, for example, that the New Testament does not tell us anything about ordination or about any office of Eucharistic presidence in the early Church should alert us to the fact that there are far more important considerations concerning Eucharist than the office of the presider and that our preoccupation with that question is perhaps excessive if not wrong-headed.[6]

Secondly, the historical facts can help to relativize convictions that have been erroneously absolutized in the course of our long history as an institution. The discovery, for example, that the New Testament witnesses to a variety of ways of organizing local churches should open our minds and hearts to genuinely ecumenical approaches to Christian communities that are not episcopal in structure. All of this amounts to saying that the establishment of historical data is a very important but preliminary step in the process of bringing the New Testament data to bear upon contemporary questions.

The second step is the use of the historical data in the difficult task of theological interpretation in which a genuine fusion of horizons, that is, of our contemporary horizon with the horizon of the earliest Christian experience, takes place.[7] Within this newly established horizon we must raise our own questions and find our own answers, answers that will be in living continuity with the revelation to which the Bible witnesses because they are articulated within the tradition that embraces the entire Christian experience from New Testament times to our own day.

C. *New Testament Data*

Let us turn now to our first two questions: On the basis of New Testament data, should women be excluded from liturgical preaching, and should liturgical preaching be restricted to the ordained?

There are two possible New Testament bases for the exclusion of women from preaching. The first is the specific injunction of Paul that women must keep silence in the churches. The second is the general competence assigned to Church authority to regulate Church life and order, including the exercise of the ministry. On the first basis, women would be excluded from preaching because they are women, and thus there could be no appeal from the prohibition. On the basis of the second, the prohibition would be valid only if it is a proper exercise of Church authority and would be in effect only as long as the competent officials wished to maintain it. Obviously, the first is the more serious in theory, even though the second might be equally intractable in practice.

It is hardly necessary to cite the famous text from 1 Cor 14:33b-35:

> As in all the churches of the saints, the women should keep silence in the churches. For they are not permitted to speak, but should be subordinate, as even the law says. If there is anything they desire to know, let them ask their husbands at home. For it is shameful for a woman to speak in church.

or 1 Tim 2:11:

> Let a woman learn in silence with all submissiveness. I permit no woman to teach or to have authority over men; she is to keep silent.

These texts have been repeatedly exegeted in the past few years, and I do not wish to repeat this work. I will merely indicate, first from a negative and then from a positive perspective, why these texts cannot be used to substantiate the exclusion of women today from the ministry of the Word in general and/or from liturgical preaching in particular.

There are several important negative considerations. The first is that scholarship has fairly well established that the text in 1 Cor 14:33-35 has been interpolated into the authentic Pauline epistle from 1 Tim 2, a pastoral epistle generally recognized as post-Pauline and much more within the Jewish tradition.[8] In other words, we are not dealing with two witnesses to the same tradition but with a rather late prohibition that probably is not traceable directly to Paul.

This conclusion seems even more likely when we consider the context within which the Corinthian text occurs. In chapter 11 of the same epistle, in the context of his remarks about proper behavior in the liturgical assembly, Paul insists on the wearing of head covering by women when they pray and prophesy (1 Cor 11:5). As André Lemaire points out, this reference seems to indicate rather clearly that women not only spoke in the liturgical assembly but, since prophets, as we know from other early texts such as the *Didache*,[9] offered the Eucharistic prayer and gave what we today call the sermon or homily, women prophets might well have filled these roles.[10]

In any case, Paul both knew about and approved of women speaking in the churches and indeed exercising both of the essential speaking roles in the liturgy: prayer and prophecy. Consequently, the prohibition of women's speaking in the churches three chapters later is either a flat self-contradiction or, much more probably, an interpolation by a later hand intending to limit the freedom women exercised, with Paul's approval, in the Corinthian church and to bring that community into line with the more restrictive practice of communities of the Jewish tradition.

This leaves us with only the passage from 1 Timothy. The concern of the Pastoral Epistles with Church order and organization is well known.[11] This does not negate their importance for us, but it does place them in a different relationship to our theological reflections. The major concern of the chapter in which the prohibition of female preaching occurs is that the members of the Christian community give no offense to the surrounding society. The author wants the community to be seen as non-controversial so that "we may lead a quiet and peaceable life" (1 Tim 2:2). The freedom claimed and exercised by Christian women could well attract scandalized attention to the community in a society in which women had no public functions and were considered legal minors.[12] The desire that Christian women not seem to be violating cultural restrictions is essentially no different from the injunctions in the same epistle that Christian slaves should be content with their station and not seek either freedom from or equality with even Christian masters (cf. 1 Tim 6:1-2). There is no more reason for us to regard the restriction of women from public functions, including preaching, as normative in perpetuity than for us to regard slavery as a divine institution.

Finally, there is the question of the theological rationale given by the author of 1 Timothy for the injunction that women keep silence in the churches. The epistle claims that women must be forever subservient to men because Adam was created first and also because Eve was deceived by the devil. This is a classic example of a kind of reasoning not uncommon in the Scriptures but which cannot be credited in our own times nor allowed to determine our attitudes or practice.

As Phyllis Trible has so well demonstrated in her book *God and the Rhetoric of Sexuality*,[13] Adam in the story of creation is not presented as the first male but as the human creature prior to the differentiation of the sexes. Even if the Genesis account were, as 1 Timothy assumes, a literal historical account of creation — which it is not — it is neither the case that man was created before woman nor that any natural superiority was thus accorded him. Despite a long history of patriarchal exegesis using this text to justify the subordination of women to men, it is simply false to claim that the Genesis text itself presents Eve as more responsible for the Fall than Adam.[14] Both were deceived, both transgressed, and both were equally held responsible by God. The author of

1 Timothy may have been convinced of his reasoning and thus of his conclusion to a perpetual inferior status for women. I am not convinced that he was not doing what preachers throughout history have done — attempting to establish the fittingness of painful restrictions or impositions by grounding them in the divine plan.

In any case, what we are dealing with in the passage from 1 Timothy and the version of it we find in 1 Cor 14 is a disciplinary regulation that forbade women to speak in church or to teach or exercise authority over men. The real reason for the prohibition was ecclesiastical expediency — the felt need to keep the Christian community from appearing socially deviant in a potentially repressive cultural and religious situation. The theological reasoning given to shore up the policy is faulty in itself and, in my opinion, cannot be used to ground contemporary policy and practice.

To conclude this consideration, we must say that in all probability women did pray and prophesy, that is, they did the equivalent of preaching in the liturgical assemblies of some of the earliest churches, and Paul, at least, approved of it. Somewhat later, for understandable reasons of expediency, this freedom of women was retrenched in some churches and eventually in all of them. The repressive discipline applied to women in this matter is no more normative for us today than the command that slaves be subservient to their masters (Eph 6:5), that men wear their hair short (1 Cor 11:14), or that women have their heads covered in church (1 Cor 11:5-10).

Let us turn now to the second possible justification for the contemporary exclusion of women from preaching, namely, the juridical argument. The classic passages from the Gospels, namely Matt 16:18-19, in which the primacy is conferred on Peter along with the power of binding and loosing, and Matt 18:18, in which the power of binding and loosing is conferred on the Christian community in the person of Jesus' earthly disciples, are legitimately invoked as justifications for an exercise of self-regulation by the Church acting through her properly appointed leaders.

In 1 Corinthians we see Paul exercising apostolic authority in relationship to the community's liturgical practices. He raises both procedural and substantive objections to the behavior of the Corinthians in regard to Eucharist. He insists on proper attire and grooming on the part of both men and women, including a decent respect for gender differences,[15] especially on the part of those taking public roles in the liturgy (1 Cor 11:2-16); in chapter 14 he gives authoritative instructions about good order in the liturgical assembly, limiting the number of people who are to speak and insisting that they do so one at a time and that what is said be either intelligible in itself or properly interpreted. In 1 Cor 11:17-34 Paul addresses the much more serious issues of charity in the community, sobriety in celebration, and personal moral conversion as absolute necessities for the proper celebration of the Lord's Supper.

In summary, the New Testament certainly grounds the legitimacy of ecclesiastical authority and its proper function not only of recalling Christians to substantive theological fidelity to the meaning of the Eucharist but also of regulating even the practical details of dress, behavior, and roles in the liturgy.

The question we have to ask today is the following: Does this legitimate authority have any limits? Does it authorize ecclesiastical authorities to forbid, in perpetuity, all exercise of certain Spirit-conferred ministerial gifts by an entire group of the faithful for theologically irrelevant reasons such as sex?

Paul did not consider it incumbent upon him to forbid the exercise of any of the charisms possessed by his enthusiastic Corinthian converts. He insisted that these gifts be exercised in an orderly manner and that their exercise never infringe on charity. But it seems never to have occurred to Paul to try to bind the Spirit. It was particularly in regard to the Word of God that Paul considered all Christians, by their very calling, to be gifted. As he says to the Colossians: "Let the word of Christ dwell in you richly, as you teach and admonish one another in all wisdom, and as you sing psalms and hymns and spiritual songs with thankfulness in your hearts to God" (Col 3:16).[16] The references to the word, singing of hymns, and thanksgiving in this passage suggest that Paul is speaking of the liturgical assembly. But whether he was referring to the Eucharistic assembly in this passage or not, it is clear that he does not make any distinctions among Christians in regard to their responsibility to proclaim the Word.

As we have already seen, the restriction of women in 1 Tim 2 was culturally motivated, despite the rather flimsy attempt to justify it by an appeal to Genesis. But the very fact that the sacred author felt compelled to justify the injunction in religious terms suggests that he was aware that he was restricting the rights of female Christians and undermining the freedom they had enjoyed up to this point in sharing in the ministry of the Word.

The early Church had a profound sense of the liberty of the Holy Spirit to do new things. The Spirit inspired the admission of the Gentiles to the faith without their submission to the Law of Moses (Acts 11:1-18). The Spirit called a ferocious persecutor of the Church to become a vessel of election for the preaching of the gospel (Acts 9:1-19). And the Spirit called women as well as men to exercise various ministries in the Church (see the list of women ministers in Rom 16 as well as in various places in Acts). The guiding principle was that the action of the Spirit was free and sovereign and that the Spirit was not to be quenched, but that everything, especially the exercise of prophecy, was to be tested so that the good might be cherished (1 Thess 5:19).

In other words, Christian freedom has a very real priority over ecclesiastical jurisdiction. The one who would restrict the freedom of a Christian has to have very good reasons for doing so, and the only such reasons we find in the New Testament are that freedom has become license resulting in immorality, that a modified restriction is necessary to ensure order, or that the exercise of a certain freedom would scandalize others. Nowhere do we find that Church authorities can canonize their personal prejudices against certain groups (indeed, the Gentile question is a stunning rejection of such an attempt) or disenfranchise them in the exercise of their Christian freedom or the gifts that the Spirit has bestowed upon them.

In summary, then, there are no convincing New Testament grounds, either theological or jurisdictional, for the exclusion of women as a group from liturgical preaching. On the contrary, there are excellent grounds for regarding such a restriction as a serious abuse of legitimate authority by those holding office in the Church.

It is even more enlightening, I think, to approach this issue positively. Are there any grounds in the New Testament for claiming that not only should women not be hampered from preaching but they should be positively encouraged to exercise this ministry? I think that there are.

The most significant evidence from the Gospels is found in the Gospel of John.[17] Two incidents, that of the Samaritan woman and the Easter appearance to Mary Magdalene, strongly suggest not only that women were called to the ministry of the Word (which is the essence of the vocation to apostleship in the language of the non-Johannine traditions) in John's community but that this vocation was understood to have been entrusted to women by the will of Jesus himself. The Samaritan woman, who brought her neighbors to Jesus by her proclamation of his messiahship (John 4:1-42), and Mary Magdalene, who received the first Easter christophany and was commissioned by the Risen Lord to announce the kerygma to the assembled disciples (John 20:11-18), are indisputable examples of women called to preach the Word.[18] One preached the gospel to the as yet unconverted and brought them to Jesus; the other announced the resurrection gospel to the believing community.

In the Acts of the Apostles and in the Pauline literature, we have several references to the exercise of the official ministry of the Word by women. There were women prophets, such as the daughters of Philip (Acts 21:9) and those mentioned in 1 Corinthians, as already noted. We know from the *Didache* that the prophets preached in the Eucharistic assembly and proclaimed the Eucharistic prayer. We have no reason to think that this activity was restricted to male prophets.

We have also the example of Prisca, who with her husband, Aquila, catechized the learned Apollos (Acts 18:24-26). And if, as has been suggested often enough, the *Iounias* (Junias) of Rom 16:7 is a female, we have an acknowledgment by Paul of a woman apostle, indeed one who was "foremost" among the apostles.[19]

Phoebe, the deacon of the church of Cenchreae, is not only a possible historical argument for the ordination of women to the diaconate but a historical example of a woman leader of a local church, a role that quite probably included preaching, especially in the Corinthian setting.[20]

In short, the Gospel of John attests to both the vocation of women to the ministry of the Word and their effective fulfillment of that vocation. The Acts of the Apostles attests to women prophets. The Pauline letters provide us with clear historical examples of women exercising the ministry of the Word as teachers and prophets. The threefold ministry of the Word — apostleship, prophecy, and teaching — was not restricted to men in the New Testament period. We can legitimately raise the question of whether the gradual retrenchment of women's participation in that ministry does not represent the very opposite of the development of doctrine. Are we not dealing here with a falling away from the gospel, historically understandable perhaps, but no longer tolerable as we come to see how contrary to the gospel the repression of women's Christian identity and mission is, and how harmful to the Church's pastoral ministry the exclusion of women's charisms actually is?

We can now look very briefly at our second question. Even if women could be ordained, thus abolishing the issue of women's exclusion from preaching, are there good New Testament grounds for restricting preaching to the ordained? In a sense, we have answered that question. We have already seen that various forms of the ministry of the Word were considered gifts of the Spirit, given to whomever the Spirit chose to give them and endowing the recipient with freedom of speech in the Christian assembly. Although by the time of the Pastoral Epistles we see a tendency to deny this freedom to women, there is no suggestion that this restriction had anything to do with the holding or not holding of community office. Indeed, as Raymond Brown points out, 1 Timothy may well suggest that women were deacons and perhaps even presbyters in the Church of the Pastoral Epistles but not allowed to preach because of the conviction of women's subordination to men.[21] Conversely, the New Testament literature testifies abundantly to the exercise of the ministry of the Word by numerous people of both sexes who held no official posts in the Church.

However, as has already been mentioned, the fact that something was or was not done in the earliest Church does not settle the question of whether it should be done today. The Christian community gradually evolved several Church orders within which various ministries were assigned to various offices. In a relatively short time one Church order emerged as paradigmatic, and eventually the Catholic pattern of the threefold hierarchy of bishop, presbyter, and deacon became universal. This order was retrospectively seen as divinely instituted and therefore unchangeable.[22]

Although many today would question this conclusion and would certainly question whether other Church orders developed in the non-Roman Christian communions should be declared contrary to or outside the divine will,[23] few would question that the development of Church order was necessary and guided by the Spirit. However in need of reform the current institution may be, institutionalization itself represents a legitimate exercise of the Church's capacity to bind and loose, to agree on and effect its own organization for the pursuit of its God-given mission in the world. This being the case, we must honestly raise the question of whether or not, as part of its legitimate institutionalization, the Church has the right to restrict the exercise of certain ministries to the incumbents of certain offices.

We must be clear in raising this question that we are talking about the restriction of the exercise of ministries, not the denial of the capacity for such ministry. As Richard McBrien aptly remarked during a recent colloquium, "Every Christian has the power to do whatever the Church is responsible to do." But radical capacity by baptism must be accompanied by personal maturity and charismatic endowment if the ministry is to be exercised competently. And all ministries in the Church must be carried out in good order. The assurance of competence and order is achieved primarily by various kinds of "licensing," of which ordination is one.

The question is not whether the Church can, and indeed should, license to preach in the Eucharistic assembly only those qualified to fulfill this ministry well. The question is whether it is a legitimate exercise of this jurisdictional authority to refuse even to examine the charismatic endowment and professional competence of most of the members of the Church, in favor of a purely juridical standard that cannot in principle guarantee either the charismatic endowment or the professional competence of the preacher and that in practice has richly demonstrated its own inadequacy.

The people of God have a right to hear the Word of God preached competently and effectively. This right has substantive and practical priority over jurisdictional arrangements,[24] the more so when these latter represent, at best, pure clericalism that has no foundation whatever in the New Testament and, at worst, a thoroughly unchristian prejudice against women.

In looking at these two questions — whether women should be excluded from liturgical preaching and whether such preaching should be restricted to the ordained — we have reached two conclusions. First, we can certainly establish that women were not universally excluded from preaching in the early Church and that when they were excluded, it was for non-theological reasons. The New Testament presents women as called to the ministry of the Word by Jesus himself and as exercising that ministry effectively in the early Church. Nonetheless, we cannot conclude that this historical data determines what Church practice in this regard must be in the contemporary Church. Similarly, we can establish that preaching was not restricted to any particular group or office in the earliest communities but was regarded as a charismatic gift to be exercised by those called and endowed by the Spirit. Nevertheless, we cannot prove that restriction of this or any other ministry is illegitimate in the later Church once a certain Church order has developed and been vindicated by the historical experience of the people of God. The passage from historical data to theological conclusions is not mechanical.

Thus, our second conclusion: The New Testament data must be used, not as so many weapons in the arsenals of opposing parties, but as indications of the deep theological and spiritual motivations that the Spirit has implanted in the Church. Among these Spirit-given treasures are:

- a far-reaching Christian freedom that must not be trammeled except for the gravest and most profoundly theological reasons (see Acts 15:1-29);
- a radical equality and unity among the children of God in Christ, in whom there are no distinctions based upon race, social station, or sex (see Gal 3:28);
- the primordial right of the community to have the Word of God preached to them in season and out of season by those most competent through charism and preparation to do so;

— the utter incompatibility of Christian community experience with any form of clericalism that would introduce
relationships of superiority or domination into the family
of God (see Matt 23:1-12; Mark 10:42-45);

— the Church's capacity to institutionalize itself for the orderly pursuit of its mission, and the Spirit-inspired resistance to the tendency of the institution to prefer itself to
the mission.

It is these theological and spiritual characteristics of the Church's
experience that come to light in our examination of the historical
practices and teaching of the early Church and that guide us, not
in slavish imitation of first-century thought and behavior, but in
seeking the proper incarnation of these values in the cultural and
religious setting of our own time. In my opinion, the exclusion
of women from preaching at the Eucharist, as well as the restriction of such preaching to the ordained, represents a betrayal of
the gospel, not only because these regulations enshrine an anti-
evangelical sexism and clericalism but also because they silence
many who are gifted and trained to preach, at a time when there
is truly a famine of the Word of God in the land.

II. New Testament Foundations for a Theology of Preaching

Let us turn now from the historical-theological question of
New Testament material related to the question of preaching by
the non-ordained and address the ultimately more significant
question: Is it possible to find in the New Testament foundations
for an adequate theology of preaching that would ground a
theologically responsible answer to the question of who should
preach in the liturgical assembly?

There is no doubt that, according to the New Testament, the
ministry of the Word is the central ministry of the Church.[25]
This may be less than obvious to some Catholics who grew up at
a time when Catholics were discouraged from personal reading
of the Bible, when the reading and preaching of Scripture in the

liturgy were seriously underemphasized, and when the sacraments were understood less as the proclamation of Good News than as quasi-magical rites. But it is clear from the Gospels that Jesus' own mission was to proclaim by word and deed the coming and presence of the reign of God (see Mark 1:14-15).

After his resurrection Jesus commissioned some of his disciples, namely, Mary Magdalene (John 20:17), the Twelve and their companions (John 20:22-23; Matt 28:16-20), and finally Paul (Gal 1:11-17) to announce the gospel, which now consisted in the Good News that God's reign had come in Jesus the Christ. As soon as the Spirit descended upon the community, Peter and his companions began to announce the Good News to all who had come to Jerusalem for the feast of Pentecost (Acts 2:1-42). The first major internal conflict of the Church, recorded in Acts 6, concerned the refusal of the Jerusalem apostles to allow other ministries, such as the distribution of alms, to distract them from their primary ministry of preaching the Word. Paul understood his vocation as a binding call to preach the gospel (e.g., Rom 1:1; 1 Cor 4:15; 9:16-17), and when he lists some of the ministerial gifts given to the community at Corinth, he ranks the threefold ministry of the Word in the first place: "God has appointed in the church first apostles, second prophets, third teachers" (1 Cor 12:28).

We find the same testimony to the primacy of the ministry of the Word in the Church's earliest catechism, the *Didache*, which dates from the early second century. This document repeatedly singles out prophets and teachers as the most essential ministers in the community, even basing the reverence owed by the community to bishops and deacons on their participation in the ministry of the prophets and teachers.[26] Even the strictures against false prophets in this document testify to the prestige of the prophetic ministry and the esteem in which it was held.

There is nothing arbitrary or mysterious in this clear priority of the ministry of the Word as the foremost exercise of the Church's mission. That mission is to be the herald, the sign, and the agent of the reign of God in this world[27] by evoking and sustaining faith in the God revealed in Jesus Christ and fostering the community of those who share that faith as they strive to further the reign of God on this earth. But faith comes through hearing, and there can be no hearing of the Word of God unless it is announced (see Rom 10:14-15). Proclaiming the gospel, therefore, is not one ministry among others but the central ministry to which the others are ordered and which gives meaning to them. Even the sacraments are, in essence, an effective proclamation of the gospel by word and action. This is why, in the early Church, it was the prophets, those whose ministry consisted in bringing the gospel into direct and effective interaction with the life of the community, who were recognized as the most appropriate persons not only to preach at the liturgy but also to offer the Eucharistic prayer of the community.[28]

The first and most fundamental form of the ministry of the Word was apostleship, even though the term "apostle," as we shall see, is not always used to describe the reality about which we are speaking. The apostle was one who, like Jesus, was sent to bring Good News to the poor. As the Father had sent Jesus primarily to the lost sheep of the house of Israel, so Jesus sent his disciples to proclaim the reign of God to all people, even to the ends of the earth and of time (see Matt 28:18-20). This vocation to apostleship, although not always designated by this term (for example, those commissioned in Matt 28:16-20 are called "disciples"), entailed both the authority and the responsibility to call people to faith by the proclamation of the gospel.

But almost immediately the ministry of the Word unfolded in the Church into the threefold ministry of apostleship, prophecy, and teaching. The apostle proclaimed the Word to those who had not yet heard it. The prophet, speaking "in the Spirit," helped believers see the immediate relevance and impact of the Word on their lives. The teacher undertook to lead believers into the deep meaning of the Word so that its full significance could be gradually assimilated and allowed to transform their minds and hearts according to the pattern of Christ crucified and risen.[29]

But because all forms of the ministry of the Word are rooted in the fundamental vocation to apostleship, we can perhaps best pursue our question about who is called to preach and according to what criteria by addressing the question of the meaning and criteria of apostleship in the New Testament.

The first apostle, as we have said, is Jesus, the one sent by the Father (see John 3:16 17 and elsewhere). The Gospels suggest, in various ways, that Jesus, even during his lifetime, shared his apostolic vocation with some of his followers. It is not the case, as some would have us believe, that participation in Jesus' apostolate was limited, during or after his lifetime, to the twelve men whom Luke tells us Jesus named "apostles" (Luke 6:13). The Gospels tell us that many people participated in Jesus' ministry of preaching by word and work, and that Jesus validated their ministry in various direct and indirect ways. He is presented as sending out the Twelve (Mark 6:7-13; Matt 10:1, 5-15; Luke 9:1-6) and later the Seventy-two (Luke 10:1-12) to preach and work miracles in his name; he tacitly sends the Samaritan woman to announce him to her townspeople and personally brings her preaching mission to a successful conclusion (John 4.4-42); he restrains his jealous disciples from impeding the miracle-working of a person who was not one of Jesus' immediate group by telling them that if the man was doing good in Jesus' name, with or without explicit authorization from Jesus, he was implicitly "for" Jesus (Mark 9:38-41) and should be left alone. However, it was only after the resurrection that Jesus directly commissioned certain chosen witnesses as apostles charged with the mission now entrusted to the Church. These original apostles involved some others in their apostolate during the first generation of the new community's existence.

The post-resurrection picture of apostleship, however, is extremely complex. It is not necessary to repeat here the painstaking research of scholars such as Raymond Brown and C. K. Barrett, who have amply demonstrated how difficult, indeed impossible, it is to establish a univocal notion of apostleship in the New Testament or to determine who, or even how many, were recognized as apostles.[30] To summarize briefly, it is evident from the New Testament that various sets of criteria for apostleship functioned in the early Church.[31] Luke, in the Gospel but especially in Acts, tends to limit apostleship to the twelve who were the companions of Jesus during his earthly life, or at least to accord them a kind of superior apostleship.[32]

But even Luke must acknowledge the apostleship of Paul (see Acts 14:4, 14), who had never known the earthly Jesus, although Luke attempts to attach Paul's apostleship in some way to that of the Twelve (Acts 9:27). Paul, who is utterly convinced of his own apostleship, claims to have been appointed to this mission by the glorified Christ who appeared to him on the road to Damascus (1 Cor 9:1; Gal 1:1). He does not dispute the apostleship of those called before him (Gal 1:17; 1 Cor 15:9), and he recognizes the apostleship of some who were appointed by or for the churches, such as Epaphroditus (Phil 2:25), Barnabas (Acts 14:14), Silas (Acts 15:40), and Andronicus and Junias (Rom 16:7), but he claims that his own apostleship, while not superior to theirs, is in no way inferior to (2 Cor 11:5; 12:11) nor dependent upon theirs (Gal 1:16-17). As we shall see, it is precisely this "independent" claim that makes the apostleship of Paul a particularly useful locus for the determination of the theological meaning of this vocation.

Although it is notoriously difficult for us to determine exactly who, or how many, among the first generation were considered apostles — and the claim was disputed even among the apostles themselves and those to whom they preached — it is not hard to understand why the issue of apostleship was so important. Apostleship was not an office in the early Church any more than prophecy or teaching was. Apostleship was a personal vocation to bear authoritative witness to that which one had personally experienced, namely, the Christ-event in Jesus of

Nazareth. The apostles were essentially those who had seen and heard, and their witness was the norm of the faith of those whom they evangelized. Their interpretation of the Christ-event was the foundation and content of the Church's faith, and, conversely, it was the Church's recognition of the fidelity of their witness to the reality of the event that established their credibility. The effort on the part of the first-generation apostles themselves and of later generations to establish criteria for deciding who was an apostle and what was genuinely apostolic teaching followed from these principles.

As the first generation of apostles, most importantly Paul, Peter, James of Jerusalem, and John, died out, the question of authoritative witness shifted from the question of personal apostleship to the question of apostolicity. In other words, the question became that of authoritative tradition. When direct appeal could no longer be made to the eyewitnesses commissioned by the Lord himself, how could the community be certain that the witness given in later and changed circumstances was substantially identical with the original kerygma?

C. K. Barrett, in an admittedly somewhat simplified schema, identifies three basic approaches to this task of discerning the apostolicity of preaching and practice in the subapostolic period.[33] We have some evidence of all three approaches in the later writings of the New Testament itself.

The first approach is the personal one, which finds the locus of apostolicity in the original apostles, the Twelve, according to Luke, and Paul, according to the Pastoral Epistles. The true tradition goes back to these first apostles, and only that is apostolic which conforms to the pattern of life and preaching that these first apostles established.

The second approach is the ecclesiastical one, which appears in Jude and 2 Peter. Official interpretation of the original witness is uniform and universally binding, and anyone who departs from the officially adopted teaching has departed from the authoritative tradition. This approach necessarily minimized the pluralism and harmonized the conflicts of the first generation (2 Pet 3:15-17), insisted on the importance of lawful authority (2 Pet 2:10a), and warned of the dangers to the faith posed by private interpretation of the Scriptures (2 Pet 1:20).

The third approach to the problem of apostolicity (we speak here of the reality of authentic tradition and teaching, not of the use of the vocabulary of "apostolicity," which seems to be deliberately avoided by the fourth Evangelist) is characteristic of the Gospel and First Epistle of John. Barrett calls it the "theological" approach, for rather than being concerned primarily with who carries or guarantees the tradition or how it is guaranteed, this approach is concerned with the "nature of the apostolic testimony, the authority inherent in it, and the transmission of that authority."[34] In other words, it is concerned with the intrinsic apostolicity of later preaching rather than with extrinsic validation.

The later Church has retained all three approaches to the discernment of apostolicity but, unfortunately, has often tended to rely more heavily on the more manageable external criteria than on the intrinsic theological ones. The personal and ecclesiastical approaches, unless subordinated to, and substantially informed by, the theological approach, can easily lead to the equation of genuine tradition with sheer repetition, the inability to discern the work of the Spirit in new circumstances, and the tendency to see office as the sole locus of true authority in the Church. What I wish to suggest is that it is just such neglect of the theological criteria of apostolicity, that is, of intrinsic authoritativeness in the proclamation of the Good News, that can lead to the *a priori* disqualification of certain persons or groups from preaching or to the restriction of preaching to officeholders, regardless of genuine theological qualifications. Put very simply, when juridical criteria supplant theological ones in the fundamentally theological matter of preaching and teaching, the ministry of the Word is subverted and its authority undermined.

Let us, then, examine the more important New Testament data on apostleship as they are understood by Paul and the reality of "apostolicity," that is, authentic tradition and teaching, as it is presented by John. Paul, the most striking apostolic figure of the first generation, was forced on more than one occasion to defend his claim to apostleship because he lacked one of the most evident external criteria, namely, association with the earthly Jesus. Paul had to establish his vocation on other grounds, and we, therefore, have some very explicit reflection, from the Apostle himself, on the criteria of apostleship.

Paul cannot appeal to a historical link with Jesus, and he refuses to allow his apostleship to depend on those who have such a historical link (see Gal 1:16-20). Paul rests his claim on three grounds. First, he was chosen and appointed by the glorified Christ who appeared to him on the road to Damascus (Gal 1:11-12). Second, he had assimilated the mystery he preached by participating in the sufferings and dying of Jesus (2 Cor 1:3-5; Phil 3:8-11) in such a way that he can validly exhort his hearers to be imitators of him as he is of Christ (1 Cor 11:1). Third, his preaching is effective, both positively in evoking faith in those whom he converts and negatively in exposing the evil of those who resist the Word (see 1 Cor 1:18; 9:2; 2 Cor 2:14-17; 3:1-3). Apostleship is not validated by office, eloquence, intellectual sophistication, or recommendation by others (see 1 Cor 1:10-2:5). It is validated intrinsically by its source in divine vocation, its realistic rootedness in the paschal experience of the apostle, and its effectiveness as Word of God.

When we turn to the Fourth Gospel, we are struck by the similarity between John's approach and that of Paul, even though John avoids the word "apostle." The fourth Evangelist, drawing on the authoritative tradition of the Beloved Disciple, who was, in all probability, not one of the Twelve though probably a companion and eyewitness of the earthly Jesus,[35] had much the same problem at the end of the first generation of Christian experience that Paul had at the beginning, namely, how to establish the authenticity and authority of the community's tradition. Like Paul, the fourth Evangelist does not ap-

peal to or for the approval of the Jerusalem apostles. Without
using the term, he claims independent apostolicity for the Beloved Disciple, the one who has seen and heard and borne a witness known to be true (see John 19:35; 21:20-24), thereby establishing an authentic tradition about Jesus and the meaning of
Christian discipleship as a response to the indwelling Lord.

John does not use the term "apostle," perhaps because by the
time this Gospel was written in the 90's the term had already
become identified with the Twelve. But he is very concerned
with the reality of apostolicity, that is, with the authority of the
community's tradition. John speaks not of "apostles" but of
"witnesses." Jesus is the first such witness, the one sent by the
Father to bear witness (John 1:18) in the world to what he has
seen and heard with God. Those who accept his witness see and
hear the Father in Jesus (John 14:9-11) and thus become, in their
turn, witnesses to Jesus (John 14:12; 15:27). And those who accept their witness, those who hear Jesus' Word in that of his
disciples (John 13:20; 17:20), are in no way inferior to those first
eyewitnesses (John 20:29). On the contrary, all those who
believe in Jesus enter into communion with those who have seen
and heard and handled the Word of life (see 1 John 2:20-25). The
authenticity of their experience of Jesus manifests itself in their
lives: in their loving others as Jesus has loved them in service
unto death (John 13:34-36; 15:12-14) and in their acceptance of
persecution and death after the pattern of Jesus' own mystery
(John 15:18-20).

The authenticity of their witness, like that of Paul, is tested
by its efficacy. If their word of witness to Jesus as Messiah and
Son of God draws others to Jesus as did the word of Andrew to
Peter (John 1:41-42), of Philip to Nathanael (John 1:45-47), of
the Samaritan woman to her townspeople (John 4:39-41), of
Mary Magdalene to the disciples (John 20:18), its validity is es-
tablished, regardless of whether the preacher is one of the
Twelve or a later Christian, woman or man, repentant sinner or
Beloved Disciple. And, like Jesus' own word, the authoritative

word of the true witness is a two-edged sword that will not only convert the hearer of the truth but will also convict those who are evil, leading them to persecute the witness (John 16:20) or to leave the community of disciples, to which they never truly belonged (see 1 John 2:19).

In summary, Paul and John are in essential agreement on the theological criteria of apostolicity, that is, of the intrinsic authority of the witness that the minister of the Word brings to event through preaching. Neither appeals to institutional approval or personal historical qualifications such as earthly contemporaneity with Jesus or membership among the Twelve. Both would have us locate apostolicity, that is, the being sent as Jesus was to preach the Good News, wherever we find a call by Christ to the ministry of the Word, personal assimilation to Jesus in his paschal mystery lived out by participation in his service and suffering, and charismatic effectiveness in evoking faith by bringing the Word to event in the lives of others.[36]

CONCLUSION

Let me draw these reflections to a close with some conclusions that might have a bearing on the contemporary question of preaching by the non-ordained. In the first part of the paper, I tried to establish that the New Testament data does not support the *a priori* exclusion of any group of Christians, such as women, from any dimension of the ministry of the Word. On the contrary, this data suggests that women were involved in this ministry from the earliest days of the Church and that their involvement was seen as willed by Jesus. Second, the New Testament does ground the legitimacy of the ordering of ministries in the Church by the competent authorities, but this administrative activity is for the sake of effective proclamation of the Word and is abused when it is used to limit unnecessarily the freedom of Christians to exercise the gifts they have received from the Spirit for the building up of the Church.

In the second part of the paper, we explored the essential intrinsic qualification for authentic preaching, namely, the authority of apostolicity. We saw that the task of discerning apostolicity it not easy. Although institutional criteria can be useful, they must not supplant the theological criteria of vocation, personal assimilation of the mystery of Christ that one preaches, and the gift of the Spirit (which must be cultivated through study and prayer), enabling the witness to bring the Word to event effectively and to evoke the crisis of faith in the hearers.

It is abundantly clear to anyone observing the current ecclesial scene that those called to the ministry of the Word are not all called to ordained ministry and that not all who are ordained are gifted for the ministry of the Word. The central concern of those who have responsibility for the ordering of ministry in the community must be that the Word not be bound or silenced for the sake of human traditions, much less for the protection of titles and first places in the assembly, but that the Word of God be preached in season and out of season until the gospel has indeed been proclaimed to every creature.

NOTES

1. "Directory for Masses with Children," Sacred Congregation for Divine Worship (*Acta Apostolicae Sedis* 66 [1974]) 30–46. R. K. Seasoltz, in *New Liturgy, New Laws* (Collegeville, Minn.: The Liturgical Press, 1980), observes that this legislation actually "grants more rights to children in regard to the homily than to adults" (p. 97).

2. For an excellent treatment of the question of the emergence of the episcopacy in the early Church, see R. E. Brown, "*Episkopē* and *Episkopos:* The New Testament Evidence," *Theological Studies* 41 (1980) 322–338. Attention should be paid especially to the method employed by Brown to relate New Testament data to later questions. This article is reprinted in *The Critical Meaning of the Bible* (New York: Paulist Press, 1981) 124–146, under the title "An Example: Rethinking the Episcopate in the New Testament Churches."

3. A very readable treatment of these questions can be found in A. Lemaire, *Ministry in the Church,* trans. C. W. Danes (London: SPCK, 1977). For those who wish to investigate the question in greater detail, see B. Cooke, *Ministry to Word and Sacraments: History and Theology* (Philadelphia: Fortress Press, 1976), especially the first chapter in each of the five parts.

4. I borrow this terminology from R. E. Brown, "The Meaning of Modern New Testament Studies for the Possibility of Ordaining Women to the Priesthood," *Biblical Reflections on Crises Facing the Church* (New York: Paulist Press, 1975) 52–55.

5. See "Declaration on the Question of the Admission of Women to the Ministerial Priesthood," especially Parts 2–4. The Declaration is readily available in English, along with an excellent collection of articles on its history, meaning, and argumentation as well as articles of commentary on the document itself and related questions, in *Women Priests: A Catholic Commentary on the Vatican Declaration,* ed. L. Swidler and A. Swidler (New York: Paulist Press, 1977) 37–49. For a counterargument, see "Women and Priestly Ministry: The New Testament Evidence" (a report by the Task Force on the Role of Women in Early Christianity), *The Catholic Biblical Quarterly* 41 (October 1979) 608–613. The scholars who prepared this study are not of the "blueprint" mentality but were attempting to reply to the biblical arguments in the Declaration on its own terms. I have argued at various times and places that this procedure can be counterproductive if it seems to accept the basic premises of the mentality in question.

6. See Cooke, *Ministry,* 525–530.

7. The term "fusion of horizons" has been most fully developed by

H. G. Gadamer, *Truth and Method* (New York: Seabury Press, 1975). Gadamer's work has been applied specifically to the question of New Testament interpretation by A. C. Thiselton, *The Two Horizons: New Testament Hermeneutics and Philosophical Description with Special Reference to Heidegger, Bultmann, Gadamer, and Wittgenstein* (Grand Rapids: William B. Eerdmans, 1980), especially ch. 11, pp. 293–326.

8. See Lemaire, *Ministry in the Church*, 35–36. See also the explanation of this text offered by P. Ellis, *Seven Pauline Letters* (Collegeville, Minn.: The Liturgical Press, 1982) 102–103, which suggests that this text is not Paul's words but Paul's citation of a letter from the Corinthians in which the latter demand that women be silenced in the churches. Paul, in this hypothesis, would be citing the words in order to disagree with them in his exclamation, "What! Did the word of God originate with you, or are you [men] the only ones it has reached?" (1 Cor 14:36). The variety of explanations of this text comes, at least partially, from the fact that it does not fit the theology of Paul even as expressed in this letter.

9. *The Didache, or Teaching of the Twelve Apostles*, X, 7. For the Greek and English text, see *The Apostolic Fathers*, trans. K. Lake, vol. I (Cambridge, Mass.: Harvard University Press, 1970) 308–333.

10. Lemaire, *Ministry in the Church*, 12–13 and 35–36.

11. For introductory material on the Pastoral Epistles, see "Pastoral Epistles," in J. L. McKenzie, *Dictionary of the Bible* (Milwaukee: Bruce Publishing Co., 1965) 644–646.

12. See E. Stagg and F. Stagg, *Woman in the World of Jesus* (Philadelphia: Westminster Press, 1978), especially Part I, pp. 13–100.

13. P. Trible, *God and the Rhetoric of Sexuality* (Philadelphia: Fortress Press, 1978) 1–30.

14. It is amusing to note that an opposite version of this "deception" argument appears in Gratian's *Decretals* (12th century) to ground exactly the same conclusion: "Adam was beguiled by Eve, not she by him. It is right that he whom woman led into wrongdoing should have her under his direction, so that he might not fail a second time through female levity" (*Corpus Iuris Canonici* I, Pt. II, C. 33, q. 5, c. 18). Apparently, no matter who was deceived, woman should pay for it!

15. See the interesting argument of J. Murphy-O'Connor, "Sex and Logic in 1 Corinthians 11:2-16," *The Catholic Biblical Quarterly* 42 (October 1980) 482–500, to the effect that the real purpose of this passage is to insist that men and women in the liturgical assembly should appear appropriately masculine and feminine respectively.

16. As L. Deiss points out in *Persons in Liturgical Celebrations*,

trans. D. Karampas, ed. C. Kelly (Chicago: World Library, 1978) 26–28, Christ entrusted the Scriptures and their understanding, not to the clergy, but to the whole Christian community, all of whose members share in the prophetic mission of Christ. The Word of God is meant to be shared and circulated among the members of the worshipping assembly.

17. I have developed this point at length in "Women in the Fourth Gospel and the Role of Woman in the Contemporary Church," *Biblical Theology Bulletin* 12 (April 1982) 35–45. See the bibliography of this article for reference to other material on the subject.

18. See my article "Apostleship of Women in John's Gospel," *Catholic Charismatic* 1 (February/March 1977) 16–20, for a fuller development of this point.

19. See the cautious suggestion to this effect by J. A. Fitzmyer in "The Letter to the Romans," *The Jerome Biblical Commentary* (Englewood Cliffs, N.J.: Prentice-Hall, 1968) p. 330, no. 138. The CBA Task Force statement is much less tentative (see p. 610).

20. Brown, "Rethinking the Episcopate," 141–142, thinks that 1 Tim 3 and 5 supply good grounds for thinking that women functioned as deacons and possibly even as presbyters in the churches of the Pastoral Epistles but that these offices did not include preaching, which is forbidden to women in 1 Tim 2:12. I wonder, however, what role a deacon or presbyter who could neither teach nor exercise authority over men would have. This anomaly only raises further questions about how absolute the silence rules were for women, even in more Jewish communities.

21. See note 20.

22. For an excellent treatment of the meaning of "divinely instituted" and the effect of this notion on the development of Church order, see J. F. McCue, "Is the Early Christian Development of Ministry Definitely Absolutized?" *Ministering in a Servant Church*, ed. F. A. Eigo and S. E. Fittipaldi (Villanova, Pa.: University Press, 1978) 19–44.

23. See Lemaire, *Ministry in the Church*, 112–117, and R. E. Brown, *Priest and Bishop: Biblical Reflections* (New York: Paulist Press, 1970) 82–86.

24. The question of the priority of the right to ministry over jurisdictional arrangements is being raised repeatedly in different theological quarters. It is usually raised in relation to the sacraments, but if what we have been saying about the centrality of the ministry of the Word in the Church's mission is correct, the same reasoning must apply in relation to preaching. On this point see the abstract "The Eucharist Today," *Theology Digest* 25 (Spring 1977) 24–31; *The Right of the Community*

to a Priest, ed. E. Schillebeeckx and J.-B. Metz, Concilium 133 (New York: Seabury Press, 1980).

25. For fuller treatment of this important topic see Cooke, *Ministry*, esp. 528–530.

26. *Didache* XV, 1-2.

27. This formulation of the Church's mission has been most clearly propounded by R. McBrien, *Church: The Continuing Quest* (Paramus, N.J.: Newman Press, 1970), esp. 67–85.

28. See *Didache* X, 7.

29. On the threefold ministry of the Word, see Lemaire, *Ministry in the Church*, 11–13.

30. See Brown, *Priest and Bishop*, esp. 47–63; C. K. Barrett, *The Signs of an Apostle* (Philadelphia: Fortress Press, 1972).

31. Barrett, *Signs*, 71–73, delineates eight different persons or groups that appear as apostles in the New Testament. Brown, *Priest and Bishops*, 48, proposes to discuss two but implies that there are others.

32. See Brown, *Priest and Bishop*, 48–50, for the broader view, and Barrett, *Signs*, esp. 47–54 for the more restrictive view.

33. Barrett, *Signs*, 74–76.

34. Barrett, *Signs*, 76.

35. This position is the most common among reputable Johannine scholars. See, for example, R. Brown, *The Community of the Beloved Disciple* (New York: Paulist Press, 1979) 31–34, who gives references to opinions of other scholars on this point.

36. It is the New Hermeneutics and its disciples that have developed the most beautiful and challenging analyses of this third characteristic. I would recommend, for an example, R. W. Funk, *Language, Hermeneutics, and Word of God: The Problem of Language in the New Testament and Contemporary Theology* (Chico, Calif.: Scholars Press, 1966), esp. 1–18.

Toward a Theology of Preaching: One Model and One Question

WILLIAM J. HILL, O.P.

This paper will attempt something quite modest, namely, to raise the question: "What is the preacher doing when he or she preaches"—that preacher to whom the community has a right (as Father Schillebeeckx told us in the first paper) and whose preaching activity is rooted in the Bible (as Sandra Schneiders has made clear in the preceding paper). Entitled "Toward a Theology of Preaching," it bears the subtitle "One Model and One Question." It is one model, because what will be suggested here is only one theory among many others, all of them legitimate and viable. Pluralism in this area derives from the fact that preaching is not akin to science but much closer to an art form, and there are no hard and fast rules dictating how the artist is to go about a task that is essentially creative. The justification for working out this one theory is the hope that, in a dialectical tension of ideas, it will suggest other viable theories. The paper poses one question, because the topic of this symposium seemingly obligates us to cast at least a sideward glance at the question of preaching by the non-ordained, in light of the theory here developed. The procedure vis-à-vis both questions will be theological, but heuristically so, that is, probing in a tentative and exploratory way.

The task of the preacher can be viewed as that of mediating a saving encounter of the believer with the living God. The locus of the encounter is, then, the Word of God seen as utterance

91

toward humankind, constituting God's sovereign and saving initiatives toward men and women. The context is an ecclesial one, for the Word of God is spoken to the Church—not to people as individuals but as persons forming the community of believers. Indeed, God's Word, in its meaning and meaningfulness, is constitutive of that community called Church. Thus, the preacher's word is the Word of God in the form of the Word of the contemporary Church. But what is this more precisely?

Some greater precision can be gained in describing preaching or proclamation as "kerygmatic re-interpretation or re-presentation."[1] The kerygma is here understood as the content of God's Word brought to language in a normative way (*norma non normata*) in the New Testament as read in the Church.[2] It is expressed foundationally in Jesus' own message, "Repent and believe for the kingdom of God is at hand" (Mark 1:15), and more proximately in the Church's message that in the life, death, and resurrection of Jesus of Nazareth, God proffered, and continues to proffer today, reconciliation and salvation to humankind. This, then, is the Word of God—the New Testament being not that Word in a self-identical way, but rather the normative literary articulation of it—wherein God, even though he must remain concealed, due to human finitude and sinfulness, nonetheless "unconceals" for us his loving intentionalities toward the world.

All of this is perhaps general enough to be beyond serious controversy. It becomes a bit more problematic with the realization that the kerygma, in spite of representing God's once-and-for-all activity that will never be surpassed, does not confront us with one monolithic meaning that needs only to be transferred unchanged into the present. It is not an objectively finished product that needs but to be translated into contemporary idiom or updated into today's cultural ambiance. The meaning of the kerygma is less something enshrined in the texts than something that comes to pass within the consciousness of the believer who reads the text as God's offer and summons to men and women of today. Such understanding does not occur apart from God's grace, and so it is an understanding indigenous to faith.

But the confession that the kerygma is true cannot be made exclusively on the claims of others. We cannot in human authenticity confess that Jesus is the Son of God merely on the grounds that the writers of the New Testament make this claim or that the Church proclaims it. Someplace in our own consciousness there must be experientially grasped truth (which thereby authenticates itself) on the basis of which the apostolic claims gain credibility and so make humanly possible the interior act of faith. The question that cannot be escaped is that of Jesus to Peter at Caesarea Philippi: "Who do you say that I am?" (Matt 16:16).

By the same token, the meaning of the Christian "facts" narrated in the New Testament is grasped by us in what is necessarily a process of interpretation. The would-be preacher brings to the text (and unless one starts here, there is no guarantee that the word spoken is indeed God's Word and not the preacher's own) his own pre-understanding, which urges on the text questions not identical with those entertained by the original author nor by subsequent generations of interpreters throughout the forging of tradition. Such pre-understanding comes out of a vast matrix of our whole experience with all the images, models, and conceptual structures in which such experiences have been reflectively interpreted, expressed, and so retained. Present experience, then — by which is meant experience of reality as it is given to us by God in both creation and redemption — enables the text to yield up nuances of meaning not explicitly grasped before.

This must be safeguarded from any fall into subjectivism or historicism, from any indiscriminate conformity to a prevailing worldly spirit, which would in effect replace the Word of God with the word of human beings. This is avoided by understanding that all newness of meaning yielded up is controlled by the text itself, in the sense that the meaning is either implicit in the text (then one is doing exegesis) or potentially there, awaiting actualization by the interpreter (then one is doing hermeneutics).

Thus, a dialectical process is at work here: we do not simply confront the past with present experience, but in a critical way we allow the past, which is both the text itself and the understanding it has received throughout tradition, to call into question our present understanding. What transpires is the opening up, not only of a world of meaning behind the text, out of which it emerges, but more. In Luther's phrase, echoed today by Hans Urs von Balthasar, it is not that we are to interpret the Word of God, but God's Word is to interpret us. But it interprets us as our situation before God differs historically and culturally from that of believers in previous epochs. Two additional safeguards might be mentioned at this point: (1) the experiences in question are not simply psychological and emotive in kind but cognitive and critical; (2) we are concerned with experiences that are not private but rather ecclesial in kind, and so subject to the judgment of the Church. They are experiences in the power of the Spirit who "breathes where he will."

Another way of saying this is to note that the Word, precisely as the Word *of God*, overarches all of history and gathers together past, present, and future into the simultaneity, and so the contemporaneity, of the eschatological moment. This means that as the preacher turns to the Word in the lingual expression it has achieved in the New Testament, what should be his interest is not its linguistic form or even specific content, but its character as God's offer and summons to men and women of today to respond in faith to his proffer of salvation. The Scriptures themselves bring this about, less by conveying to us some specific content than by initiating us into dialogue with their own subject matter (to borrow a thought from Hans-Georg Gadamer), which is God in his saving activity. Our disposition in approaching the texts is one of openness to the call of God, which, being oriented to the open future, cannot be predetermined, but which sounds through the received text.

The text is important because at the same time we are dealing with a Word that is spoken to people and as such must be uttered historically — that is to say, from within a given moment of human history — if it is to be humanly intelligible. Thus, salvation for the Christian is focused on the concrete events that constitute the human life and death of Jesus, and on the disciples' experience of his resurrection. These come to us in the narratives of the New Testament, which are already the interpretations by the disciples of their own experience of these events. As the New Testament articulates their experience in its cultural form, so our own understanding is an articulation of our differing experience of these selfsame events. An important difference, of course, is that our experience is mediated by theirs. But it is possible to say that our encounter with the living God, mediated by the text in its objectivity, occurs not only within experience but precisely as interpreted experience.

At this point a caution must be expressed. The task of the preacher is here viewed as one of reinterpreting the content of God's Word on the basis of present-day experience. This is legitimate, with the understanding that underlying the language of the New Testament are the experiences of the evangelists (including, of course, such writers as Paul), to which they give expression in the religious culture of first-century Palestine and the surrounding Hellenic world. This awareness affords us the hermeneutical key for interpreting our own contemporary experiences, in the cultural categories of the modern world, as instances of God's continuing offer of salvation to us.

This means that the experiences wherein we encounter God are in fact experiences of grace, as were those of the inspired writers. They are not *merely* human engagements with the world (whether of nature or of humankind), which are then interpreted only rationally, and so are no more than projections of finite humanity. They do occur primarily as human exchanges transpiring on a horizontal level of existence, but they constitute an experience of reality that amounts to a basic form of revelation. God manifests his presence and his summons in and through the structures of the real, both cosmic and cultural-historical.

Religious experience is thus not some isolated sphere of experience, but is a depth-dimension to ordinary experience. But such experiences manifest the divine only insofar as they are interpreted experiences. There are no "raw" experiences that amount to direct discoveries of God apart from an interpretive element. By this is meant neither an interpretation that is subsequent to the experience, superimposed on it from without, nor one that works *a priori*, determining in advance the meaning of the data, but an interpretation intrinsic and indigenous to the experience, forming a dimension of the experience itself.

This is the context of revelation, not because of the experien*cing* as such, but because of *what is experienced* in its objectivity over and against all activity of human subjectivity. It is the phenomena themselves, in their own intrinsic meaning and meaningfulness, as resistant to controlling knowledge on our part, that enables them to mediate God and God's will to men and women. At the same time, this is revelatory occurrence only insofar as it is interpreted, because interpretation in this sense is really a response in faith to God's "unconcealing" of himself through the realities of world and history wherein he draws near to us. This is a faith-act and not one of reason alone, because it is a response to the experience of grace, of God proffering salvation to men and women today. In Schillebeeckx's phrase (to whom much of the thinking here developed owes its inspiration), it is an awareness that runs through whatever we experience, pointing to the fact that God has made the cause of humankind to be God's own cause.[3] It is the surrender to truth that gives itself through human rationality but lies itself beyond the grasp of purely rational processes. However, interpretation of this sort, ultimately controlled by the interpreted, has its own history preserved and passed on in living tradition.

What is at work here, then, is a dialectical process. The confessional historical faith in Jesus of Nazareth on the part of those of us who feel constrained to preach is the enabling factor in our interpretation of present experiences as themselves revelatory. Yet, simultaneously, that interpretive experience enables us to reinterpret the kerygma as God's saving activity toward us today and, in so doing, to add to the narration that constitutes tradition.

The significance of all this for preaching is that experience readily gives rise to conviction and certitude, due to its self-authenticating character. The experiencer spontaneously seeks to give utterance to what he or she has encountered in experience as a witness to it. This is to say that the very experience as something human is bound up with language, indeed becomes itself a speech-event. The experiencer thus becomes a communicator seeking to draw others into the circle of new understanding that constitutes a faith-response to the encounter with God. The experience thus assumes a narrative structure. Preaching is less the explanation of dogmas or doctrines — necessary as the latter are — than the recounting of a narrative, with all the dramatic implications of bringing to the fore what Johannes-Baptist Metz calls "dangerous memories,"[4] and the urging upon the listener of a decision either for or against Jesus as the Christ of God. Putting this into a larger context, the preacher incorporates the articulation of his or her own new experiences of God's grace into the ongoing narrative that already constitutes living tradition, thereby creatively augmenting that tradition.

This narrative would appear to have two foci, or to unfold in a dipolar way. On one hand is the christological focus, for the narrative is the recounting of God's rescue of us in the story of Jesus' human life. On the other hand is the pneumatological, for all genuine proclamation is done in the power of the Spirit. By this is meant the Holy Spirit (*Pneuma Hagion*) who is the Spirit of Jesus crucified and raised, yet at the same time is very God dwelling within us as our spirit, when, as in St. Paul's phrase, he "lays fast hold upon us." It is the Spirit who inaugurates our experiences of grace, enabling us to believe — not only in summoning us to belief but also in answering that summons within us.

The Spirit, however, is characterized by a certain anonymity; he has no doctrine of his own but "will remind you of all I have said to you" (John 14:26). He conceals himself, as it were, behind the Word who is personally God's self-expression and who has become visible to us in our own flesh. The initial disposition, then, of the would-be preacher is one of surrender to the Spirit who must "not be quenched" (1 Thess 5:19). It is, in short, conversion, in the sense of that about-face which the New Testament calls *metanoia*.

This reception of the Spirit is at once gift and task. It is God's unexacted grace, but at the same time it is, for those in whom it occurs, a summons to the mission of witnessing in word and deed to the saving act of God. Thus, the appearances of the Risen Christ in the New Testament — which, however they are explained, occur in the power of the Spirit — are never without this calling of the disciples to a ministry of the Word. The ever-new meanings of God's Word, then, to which the Spirit grants entrée are, by a dynamic of their own, communicable to others and constitutive of community on the part of those who hear and, in hearing, believe.

This role of the Holy Spirit in forming the community of belief through the Word brings to center stage the work of those who proclaim that Word. What preaching seeks to achieve is not an institutional or ecclesiastical restructuring (necessary as the need for reform may be), not biblical fundamentalism (which fails to take into account the revelatory character of present experiences), not an exclusively charismatic piety (which runs the risk of being merely private, of saying "yes" to Jesus while remaining resistant to the Church as the community of the Spirit); rather, preaching seeks to achieve the ecclesial reality of a Church truly given over to following after Christ, to seeking ever greater conformity to him and the evangelical values lived by him in his human life. Once again, this is something rooted more in praxis than in theory. But for it the Church needs leaders, and it is here that the role of the preacher is defined; it is to this that the consciousness of the preacher lends itself.

From this it would seem that the primary obligation to preach belongs to those who hold the office in the Church: bishop, priest, deacon, or minister of the gospel. But Christian proclamation is truncated and impoverished if such ministerial preaching is not complemented by a vital lay preaching movement alongside it.

Significant here is a special obligation, not grounded in office at all but entirely charismatic in origin, on the part of those who belong to religious orders whose work is apostolic and extends in one way or another to proclamation. The character of preaching here assumes a difference at least in mode. All preaching is Christocentric, and all Christologies acknowledge in some sense the primacy of praxis over theory. But for those who live according to the vows of the religious life, this primacy takes the form of a radical following after Christ. Such Christians, to take one example, are impelled through a vow of poverty to a solidarity with the poor and to a life of witnessing against the tyranny of possessions and the self-assertiveness that motivates it.

Here a concrete way of following after Christ, to the extent that it is genuine, nuances the preaching that it nurtures. Simply put, such preaching acquires a prophetic character precisely because of the style of life out of which it proceeds — one that seeks to correspond in visible and symbolic ways with the radical demands of the gospel. This characteristic is less possible for the institutional Church, which cannot so easily depart from the standards of the secular sphere. Thus, the various forms of religious life tend to exist on the outer peripheries of the institutional Church, with an unavoidable tension between them and the domesticated Church. By and large, however, this would appear as a healthy tension.

Be that as it may, the present state of preaching seems to be one of crisis, something not at all unusual in times of major transitions. One way of coming to grips with it is to see it as a crisis of credibility, a lack of deep interiorized belief on the part of large segments of the supposedly Christian populace that forms the preacher's audience.

Karl Marx urged his disciples to leave religion alone (by which he meant primarily Christianity), on the grounds that it would soon vanish of its own failed momentum as Marxist societies superseded it. Time has proven Marx to have been very much mistaken. Concern for the God of Jesus refuses to go away. This may point to the fact that the crisis of credibility is not really a crisis of faith but one of culture, that is, one of communicating the Good News in a radically changing cultural context.

I suspect that people *want* to believe but find the form in which the message is preached alien to their own experiences. Thus, the task of preaching becomes one of forging a new language that is appropriate to those experiences in their revelatory power, without neglecting the normative role of Scripture and tradition. Jean Paul Sartre has come close to the mark, perhaps, with the devastating criticism that Christianity discredits itself because it makes no difference in the quality of life. Historically, Christians have been quite as responsible for unleashing evil upon society as have non-Christians. Part of the difficulty, at any rate, may be that the way in which Christianity is presented, the mode of its proclamation, has rendered it meaningless in its power to confront present problems.

God is not dead, but it is hard to deny that God is absent from contemporary culture. It is possible that we have been looking for God in the wrong places. What the preacher seeks to discover and to convey, though it is something specifically Christian, is to be found *within* the world rather than outside of or above it. Is not this where the Spirit operates in seeking out men and women, that is, in this secular world even in its very secularity — granted that what is sought there is the Transcendent, concerning whom clues are discoverable only at a certain depth dimension of such ordinary experience? If so, effective preaching will not take place under the misguided notion of fostering escape from the world, for it is precisely from within the prevailing human situation that one will listen for the voice of the Spirit.

On the preacher's part, this reality means that a certain solidarity with a wounded world bearing the marks of evil and suffering is required. This view of things is confirmed in the faith-act. Experiences are by definition always contemporary, for they are an awareness of something in its very presence to the subject knowing and so responding in love or in the refusal to love. This is faith in a basic sense as trust that truth lies implicit in the phenomena that confront us as reality given by God, especially insofar as such phenomena are not subject to our manipulations. To use an apt phrase of *Gaudium et Spes* from the Second Vatican Council, "God reveals himself by revealing man to himself."[5]

The very emphasizing of this truth, however, prompts a caution regarding its understanding and application. Much of the preacher's concern is with restoring life to a Church that has over-adapted to the world and its structures. The life in question here is something specifically Christian: the "new creation" won for us by Jesus in his dying and rising, and lived by us in the Spirit. If this life is mediated to us in no way other than through worldly realities, it cannot be derived nor inferred from human capacities and achievements. It is always life in response to God's unexpected offer of love, which, even while mediated through others, always remains grace from the Spirit. This calls for an attitude of critical negativity toward the structures and the spirit of secular existence, avoiding all conformity to the mores of bourgeois society and conventional piety in the forgetfulness that we are a people of unfulfilled promise. There can be no collapse of faith into ideology, no absolutizing of finite structures of whatever sort, including the ecclesiastical. All such retain a provisionary character.

Another way of putting this is to allow that the prophetic character of preaching bespeaks an element of urgency that attends it. Now is the time, the *kairos;* every moment is potentially the eschatological moment in which salvation is offered us. It is awareness of this that the preacher seeks to awaken in us. And it is what led Luther to view preaching as a sacrament.

We can even say that the preacher functions in imminent expectation of the Parousia; there is a sense in which the Second Coming is already at hand, summoning those who hear God's Word to decision here and now. This forestalls giving to the present order of things a power it does not have. We cannot remain captive to the past, granting our historicity (though it is there in tradition that preachers find their own identity and that of the communities they address), nor so oriented to the future as to empty the present of all meaning other than that of being a stepping-stone to the future.

Christian preaching remains aware of the transitory character of contemporary existence and so seeks the transcending and thus perduring dimension of present life. This is to acknowledge that eternal life is not some mode of duration that merely succeeds temporal duration. Rather, it is the full fruition of what is begun in this temporal existence, the consummation of the self-enactment we are even now achieving in earthly existence. Thus, it is the kingdom of God already inaugurated within our history but unable to reach consummation except beyond the boundaries of history.

One obvious reaction to this way of viewing the preaching act is that it tends to confuse preaching with theology, especially in light of the dominant tendency nowadays to understand theology and its method as basically hermeneutics. Preaching then appears as a sort of short-circuited theological act that moves directly from hermeneutics to communications, from Bernard Lonergan's second functional specialty to the eighth and last of them. To this it must be said that preaching cannot be reduced to a truncated theology. It is much more than a popular presentation of theological views and conclusions. The hermeneutics at work in theology is markedly critical in kind, while that entered upon in service of preaching is more existential and experiential.

The priority of praxis over theory is more obvious in preaching, as is the avoidance of technical language proper to theology. The Christocentric element, while proper to both endeavors, engages the preacher less as a Christology of *thinking about* Christ than as a Christology of *following after* Christ. I would be reluctant to suggest that ongoing conversion is less necessary for the theologian than for one entrusted with preaching; but conversion for the former serves as reflective understanding, whereas it is more immediately oriented toward witness on the part of the preacher.

One consequence of this is that in an age wherein theological pluralism is a *fait accompli,* the preacher is not constrained to commit himself or herself to any one theological system. For example, he or she can view the experiences of grace as fulfillments of an *a priori* structure to human beingness (as does Karl Rahner), or one can choose to view them as "contrast experiences" of suffering and evil that disclose God as opposing all such abuses of the human (as does Edward Schillebeeckx). The preacher can reflect on incarnational theology, stressing the manifestations of God within the *humanum,* or favor an eschatological theology that prefers to emphasize the hiddenness of God and so the negativities and discontinuities within the human realm. Or the preacher can focus, now on one, now on the other, whichever best serves the point he or she is making.

Nonetheless, granting that preaching cannot be reduced to theology, it remains true that the tie is, or should be at any rate, very close. Quite simply, theology is necessary for preaching — if not in the preacher himself or herself (which would be the ideal case), at least in the ecclesial community. At the very least, theology nurtures preaching and gives it a critical base it lacks of itself. Heinrich Ott, in a surprising synthesis of Barthian theology and later Heideggerian philosophy, has concluded, against Rudolf Bultmann, that the continuity here is such that dogmatics constitutes the reflective part of preaching. It might not be claiming too much to conceive of preaching both as a terminal "moment" in theology and as an instance of Christian orthopraxis that serves as a source for theology as theory.

Preaching and the Non-Ordained

What has been attempted here is the working out of one viable theory as to the nature of preaching, one that seeks a common element in all preaching because it acknowledges at the very outset that preaching assumes a variety of forms. Of itself, it is a notion of Christian proclamation as an activity springing from baptism and intensified by confirmation. Though it bespeaks recognition and acceptance on the part of the believing community, it remains indifferent to the question of ordination on the part of those who discharge this ministry. So conceived, there are no grounds for excluding the non-ordained from preaching. The sole prerequisite, apart from competency, is faith in God's Word attested to by baptism. On this basis Paul can write that for those "baptized in Christ . . . there are no distinctions between Jew and Greek, slave and free, male and female, for all are one in Christ Jesus" (Gal 3:28). Insofar as all Christian proclamation retains a priestly character, this truth derives from the priesthood of the faithful; it belongs to the Church in a collegial way and is shared by all believers.

Nonetheless, preaching is an innately ecclesial act (by which is meant something other than ecclesiastical). This is so because Christianity is itself indigenously communal, being a relationship to the Father through the Son and in the Spirit, which on the horizontal level opens out to all people, since the salvific will of God is universal. A succinct way of saying this is to observe that we can love God only in loving our neighbor. This community is at heart Eucharistic. This is to say that the Church is constituted precisely in the gathering of the members around the altar with the bishop or priest in celebrating and so making present, symbolically or sacramentally, Christ in his saving activity. But there is no Eucharist without a minister, whose office cannot be dismissed as a merely functional role, exercised in an *ad hoc* capacity (setting aside the possibilities in an emergency situation). Rather, the minister is understood as one responding to a call from Christ, but one mediated through the Church, which in recognizing the authenticity of the call confers upon such a one the office of exercising leadership within the community.

In a gradually developing but unbroken tradition, the Church has understood this office as that of the presbyter-bishop and, associated with him, the presbyter and the non-presbyter deacon. The presbyter, while not originally seen as a priest, came to assume that role very early in the Church. The presbyteral role is clearly one of leadership based on office, and the Second Vatican Council has explicitly stated that primary in that leadership role is the ministry of the Word.[6] Subsequent to that is mentioned the administration of the sacraments, in which consecration of the Eucharistic bread and wine holds first place. But the two are intimately connected, insofar as each achieves a presence of God in Christ — the first in the mode of the proclaimed Word, the second in the mode of shared bread and wine.[7] In this sacrament of unity, which the Eucharist brings about in the very act of symbolizing it, there is a certain fittingness — liturgical at least — in the homilist being the celebrating priest. Seemingly, the one who breaks the Word in the symbols of our languages should be the one who renders the saving event proclaimed present in the new symbols of bread to be eaten and wine to be drunk.

Thus, while preaching does not demand the sacrament of orders, it does seem to possess a certain intensity when it is discharged within the context of Eucharistic worship, and in virtue of the priestly office rather than charismatically. That the priest preaches effectively only with the help of grace, however, cannot be denied.

But this is, by no stretch of the imagination, to suggest that only the ordained should preach. It is only to imply that one form of preaching, that is, that of the homily within the Eucharist, is normally reserved to the ministry of the priest. But this is a special priesthood that has meaning only in relation to the priestly people who form the Church. Strictly speaking, the uniqueness of Christ's priesthood, the new priesthood of which we read in the Letter to the Hebrews, does away with all other priesthoods. The Church in a corporate way participates in that priesthood, and the special ministerial priesthood is derivative from, expressive of, and an instrument of, that one ecclesial priesthood. Thus, preaching is the rich agency it is because it is the prerogative of *all* Christians.

The theory of preaching espoused in the first part of this paper would have it that Christian proclamation is truncated and impoverished if the ministerial preaching is not complemented by a vital lay preaching movement alongside it. The explanation for this is, once again, simply the origin of genuine preaching out of experiences that include a revelatory dimension, so that a rich realm of Christian understanding is left to lie fallow if experiences unavailable to the priest do not find their way into Christian speech. This is more true today than ever, for it can no longer be presupposed that the layman or laywoman is a theological illiterate. Thus, especially today should ministry of the Word be more broadly based, drawing on creative contributions coming from non-clerical members of the Church who are involved in secular structures and have experiences and expertise lacking to the ordained minister. Such lay preaching would largely be done outside the Eucharistic context, in, for example, retreat conferences. But surely no major problem is involved in allowing such proclamation within the liturgy on such special occasions as funerals, wedding anniversaries, Masses for children, etc.

A quite different solution has been suggested by some who maintain that those who preach charismatically, rather than in virtue of holding office, already exercise leadership in the local church and on such grounds should be ordained and thus authorized to confect the Eucharist.[8] But this would seem to enhance an already discredited sacerdotalism or clericalism. Even if the ordination were to the diaconate, it would still perpetuate a view of the clergy-laity distinction in hierarchical terms. Once again, the lay ministry would be obscured or supplanted by a clericalized ministry; the risk would be that of the laity once again becoming passive in the Church.

This conclusion seems to gain confirmation in light of present unrest over the question of ordaining women. (This may be opening a Pandora's Box, but it can hardly be avoided.) If preaching as such does not arise out of office in the Church, then obviously women can preach, as in fact they are now doing. The current situation is simply an instance of women assuming, or reassuming, an active role in the mediation of salvation — something that has ample scriptural warrants. One need only recall Deborah or Judith or Esther in the Old Testament; and Priscilla (Acts 18:26) or Tabitha (Acts 9:36) or possibly Lydia in the New Testament.

But should women perform such ministry (of which preaching is perhaps the prime instance) in the capacity of priests? Should they in fact receive ordination? I would take it that the question as to whether this is *possible* has already been settled. There is no ontological barrier; nothing in the beingness of priesthood and that of womanhood renders them mutually exclusive. Further, there appears to be near consensus among the exegetes that no prohibition from divine positive law is to be found in the New Testament. There is a prohibition in ecclesiastical positive law, reiterated in the 1976 document from the Congregation for the Doctrine of the Faith. Can this be rescinded? In principle, yes! But should it be? What remains then is the question of *opportuneness.*

It can at least be asked if there does not still prevail a kind of incompatibility between the priesthood as presently conceived and the reality of womanhood. The Eucharistic minister from as early as the late third century has been viewed in Catholic thought as a priest, that is, as a cult figure mediating salvation in the context of worship, especially that of sacrifice. Perhaps tradition need not have developed this way, but in fact it did. And there is no question here of any priesthood other than Christ's own. But the presbyters of the early Church did come to be looked upon, not only as representatives of the believing community before God, but also as representatives of Christ vis-à-vis his holy people.

What this gives rise to *symbolically* — and we are in the realm of symbols because we are speaking of a sacrament — is a notion of hierarchy, of the agent of the cultic act having a sacral status and thus standing over against, as it were, the beneficiaries of the cultic act. If women were to be made clergywomen, would not this deprive the community of the precise contribution that might be expected from one who is human in a womanly mode and who is able to preach out of just such experiences, one who is able to give expression to ministry, for instance, less as a matter of hierarchy and rank and more as a service of love? Or, to put this in its symbolic context, women would symbolize, not the communication of the *means* of salvation, but total openness toward, and receptivity of, the *reality* of salvation.

If there is any validity to this distinction, then perhaps the time is not yet opportune for ordination of women. It would be necessary, seemingly, to wait for a massive rethinking of what office in the Church really should be. Ordination of women would mean a radical change in the symbol system that has prevailed in Christianity until now. Such a change can only come about culturally and slowly; it cannot be artificially coerced, though this is not to say that the Church does not have the obligation to point the way in light of new ministries which have already sprung up and for which the Church needs to provide structures.

Some recognition and reception by the community does

seem called for. Perhaps ordination to the diaconate is a temporary answer, but if so, there is reason for opening it up to women who already give evidence of receiving and responding to graces of leadership in the community. As for now, all that can be said, perhaps, is that we need to wait upon the Spirit, who is leading us into new experiences revelatory of God's loving will. Change will in all probability occur in small sociological units of believers constituting what is meant by local churches.[9] It is seemingly here that the Church would engage creatively in what Anne Carr calls "engendering the future."[10] But "the Spirit must not be quenched," and so God may surprise us. We may discover that even in Christian ministry, fullness of humanity demands both men and women.

NOTES

1. See W. J. Hill, "Preaching the Word: The Theological Background," *Proceedings of the Catholic Theological Society of America,* 1973, pp. 167–180; and "Preaching as a 'Moment' in Theology," *Homiletic and Pastoral Review* (October 1976) 10–19.

2. First Vatican Council (Denzinger-Schönmetzer 3006–3007).

3. Edward Schillebeeckx, *Jesus: An Experiment in Christology,* trans. Hubert Hoskins (New York: Crossroad Publishing Co., 1979) 62.

4. J.-B. Metz, *Faith in History and Society,* trans. David Smith (New York: Crossroad Publishing Co., 1980) 200f.

5. Second Vatican Council, Pastoral Constitution on the Church in the Modern World, no. 41.

6. ". . . priests as co-workers with their bishop, have as their primary duty the proclamation of the gospel of God to all" (Decree on the Ministry and Life of Priests, no. 4).

7. The Second Vatican Council speaks of multiple eucharistic presences of Christ. Basically these can be reduced to his presence (1) in the gathered community; (2) in the proclaimed Word; (3) in the consecrated bread and wine.

8. See Joseph A. Komonchak, "'Non-Ordained' and 'Ordained' Ministers in the Local Church," *The Right of the Community to a Priest,* ed. E. Schillebeeckx and J.-B. Metz, Concilium 133 (New York: Seabury Press, 1980) 44–50.

9. This is the thesis developed by William R. Burrows, *New Ministries: The Global Context* (Maryknoll, N.Y.: Orbis Books, 1980).

10. Anne Carr, "The Church in Process: Engendering the Future," *Women and Catholic Priesthood: An Expanded Vision,* ed. Ann Marie Gardiner (New York: Paulist Press, 1976). The author advocates the theory that if the Church were to reverse itself courageously and ordain women, that in itself would transform the priesthood from its present cultic role into one of a ministry of service.

The Baptismal Roots of the Preaching Ministry

MARY COLLINS, O.S.B.

Introduction

It is the common opinion of theologians and the general understanding of Roman Catholic clergy and laity that the sacrament of orders provides the basis for the preaching done in the Church. Correspondingly, it is commonly believed that the baptized members of the Church lack the radical capacity necessary for the full ministry of the Word. One investigator, R. T. Hanley, looking at the ordinary magisterium of the popes right up to the Second Vatican Council, says that the witness has remained constant: "Although it cannot be ascertained from the writings of the modern popes [Pius X to John XXIII] just what might be the precise nature of the existing relationship between the sacerdotal character and the preaching of the word, nevertheless such a relationship is readily inferred from their statements."[1]

That same writer, investigating the common teaching of twentieth-century theologians, noted a similar consistency among them. But he makes a significant judgment: ". . . it must be admitted that the nature of the existing bond between preaching and sacred Orders is in too embryonic a state of theological development to allow for a definite satisfactory solution at the moment."[2]

Hanley completed his work in 1964. Today, the notion of the bond between orders and preaching is still in force, as it has been since the eleventh or twelfth century, and it continues to be more the subject of assertion than of investigation since the Council of Trent anathematized anyone who would say that all Christians have the power for the ministry of the Word.[3] Nevertheless, the consequences of the assertion serve the Church poorly at the end of the twentieth century. This fact alone should make it a subject for serious critical scrutiny.

Some theological refinements in the assertion of a bond between ordination and preaching have indeed been made, but the practice of lay preaching is still regularly attended to in sacramental theology as an exception to the basic position that those in holy orders are the ones equipped for the full ministry of the Word in all its forms: evangelization, catechesis, exhortation, and the liturgical homily. Exceptions are popularly explained on the basis of what may be familiar as Catholic action theology, which asserts that the hierarchy may, on its initiative, delegate extraordinary powers to selected laity to participate in the ministry of the Word—at least to evangelize, catechize, and exhort. Deputing the non-ordained to preach in the liturgical assembly has been more problematic within this Catholic action scheme. Some say that such delegation is impossible in the nature of the case, since action in a sacramental setting requires sacramental power. Others point to cases where the non-ordained have done liturgical preaching and done it effectively, and conclude that it must, in the nature of the case, be possible.

Eusebius is the mentor of all those who take an empirical approach to the matter. In his *History of the Church* (6:19), written in the first half of the fourth century, he notes that a bishop of Alexandria had claimed that "it was an unheard-of, unprecedented thing that where bishops were present laymen should preach." The bishops of Jerusalem and Caesarea called their Alexandrian brother's statement "glaringly untrue," pointing to at least three cases where holy bishops had called on laity to preach, and then concluding, "Probably there are other places too where this happens unknown to us."[4]

Operating in our twentieth-century discussion, if apparently not at issue with Eusebius and the bishops whose controversy he reports on, is a mystique of spiritual sacerdotal power. Hanley, cited earlier on the common teaching and common opinion of the bond between orders and preaching, noted a recurrent language pattern in the discussion, namely, references to a "sacred fitness" and also to a "special power of the Holy Spirit" available to the ordained through an "indelible character making him, as it were, a living image of the Savior."[5] A special power, a sacred fitness, an indelible character, a living image of the Savior—this language sustains a mystique within the Roman Catholic Church to the measure that it is posited, repeated, and internalized, but not examined. It provides a framework for a worldview that diminishes the identity of those who enjoy the grace of holy baptism, while enhancing and exalting those Christians who enjoy the grace of holy orders. What does the language mean, and in what context is it intelligible?

In this short presentation, I will pursue only the matter of the theological language of a sacred fitness and of the special power of the Holy Spirit that confers the living image of the Savior. I will show that this technical language of the theological and magisterial traditions is originally liturgical language and that, as such, it is incomprehensible when, as technical language, it becomes cut off from its original liturgical matrix, the assembly of the believing community celebrating Christian baptism. The use of the language "sacred fitness," "power of the Holy Spirit," and "living image of the Savior" to refer to the ordained is secondary and derivative in the prayer life of the Church. When it is used by either the magisterium or the theological community to assert exclusive claims for the ordained at the expense of the Christian identity of the laity, it may also be ideological.

This line of investigation will bring us to the point where we can and must question the assertion that the sacrament of holy orders is the adequate foundation for the ministry of the Word, and acknowledge, rather, that it is in holy baptism that the

Church can recognize the radical capacity and the fundamental imperative for the preaching ministry. The preaching of the non-ordained may be problematic for the Church at the end of the twentieth century; but it is not accurate to say that the root of the problem is in some radical spiritual incapacity of the baptized. The unbroken tradition of the praying Church knows differently.

Theology and the Liturgical Tradition

The liturgical tradition of the Church, that is, the Church's actual way of celebrating its living faith in its identity and mission, can be called the Church's sacramental praxis, in the language of contemporary theology. The Church's liturgy is at one and the same time symbolic behavior that enfleshes doctrine, and symbolic vision that judges ecclesial life and institutions. This sacramental praxis of the liturgical assembly ought properly to provide the empirical data for systematic sacramental theology. It is *theologia prima*, primary source for *theologia secunda*, or systematic theology. Unfortunately, much of the work of systematic sacramental theology has failed to take account of the public prayer of the Church. It has overlooked it as irrelevant or dismissed it as non-data because aspects of the living tradition of worship have simply not fit into favored conceptual schemes. Such selectivity in dealing with the data of the tradition of public prayer has contributed to the present theological impasse in the matter of whether the authentic sacramental foundation for the ministry of preaching is ordination. The Church's faith is fuller and deeper than what has been given systematic form since the twelfth century.

The Church's liturgical tradition shows that the original insight into notions of sacred fitness, empowerment by the Holy Spirit, and transformation into the living image of the Savior arose in the context of celebrations of Christian baptism. The original insights were embodied in ritual language, which is not abstract and discursive but allusive and expressive.

The language of liturgical rites may lack the precision of the analytic language of systematic theology, but it does not lack cognitive content. On the contrary, the meaning of the language used in the celebration of baptism was so forceful in the first millennium that Alcuin, advisor to the Emperor Charlemagne in the eighth century, was troubled by the gap he saw growing between the faith the Church expressed in the rites of Christian initiation and the actual conditions of ecclesial life in the Frankish realm. His solution was not to bring the liturgy into conformity with the "real world" of ecclesial life, but to ask Charlemagne to back a pastoral program that would give substance to the faith of the Church regarding the identity and mission of the Christian.[6] He did not get what he asked for; the forces of history were against him. But the liturgy of baptism has remained a constant, if eccentric, witness to what is possible, normal, and indeed normative for the laity in ecclesial life.

Selected Witness from Two Centuries

Two moments will be considered here from the unbroken witness that it is God's deed at baptism which confers a sacred fitness, makes believers into images of the saving Lord Jesus, and empowers them to proclaim the gospel. The first testimony, that of the baptismal liturgy of the Frankish realm of the eighth century, Charlemagne's world, shows a high doctrine of baptism in a highly elaborated liturgical language that is at no small distance from the actual facts of ecclesial life. It is a witness from a Church faithfully handing on the mystery it had received despite the tension between liturgical celebration and ecclesial life. The second witness, St. Cyril's reflection on the baptismal praxis of fourth-century Jerusalem, speaks of a moment when there is a notable correspondence between the faith celebrated and the ecclesial life lived.

Before we look directly at this *theologia prima*, one further note is in order concerning the nature of these sources and the necessarily selective use of them here. In this discussion, reference to the baptismal liturgy extends not to the water bath only, or even to the water bath, chrismation, and first Eucharist — the so-called Easter sacraments — but also to all the liturgical celebrations that surround them — those of Holy Week, which anticipate them, and those of the Easter season, which consolidate, refine, elaborate, and confirm their meanings. The parts of a liturgical rite have their fullest intelligibility only in the context of the whole. This liturgical whole has its greatest intelligibility only in the context of the ecclesial community whose life of faith is being celebrated. That, too, will enter into our consideration.

My method of approach to the witnesses was to question them on their references to the Church's belief in "sacred fitness," "empowerment by the Holy Spirit," and "transformation into the image of Christ." This language was made the subject of scrutiny because it is part of the language subsequently taken up by systematic theology to make claims about the special identity of the ordained and to explicate the special connection between orders and the preaching ministry.

Charlemagne's Realm. In the Frankish baptismal liturgies of the eighth century, we see the Church entertaining an already traditional metaphor of "garment" as a way of getting hold of the meaning of baptism in humanly comprehensible terms. The wordplay in the English language on *suit*ability and *fitt*ingness is similar to the wordplay in Latin. Someone or something that was *habilitatus* was clothed, or equipped, or suited, or outfitted for a role or function. The Latin word *habilitatus* yields the English-language concept of ability, suggesting a correspondence between one's *out*fits and one's *inner* habits. But such abstraction is not the mode of ritual language, which prefers to allude to meaning. In the Frankish baptismal liturgy, the garment metaphor alludes to the mysterious act of God on behalf of the newly baptized.[7]

The Gallican baptismal liturgies proclaim the Church's faith that baptism habilitates, or better, rehabilitates, because of the

Spirit's work. If the baptized are divested of the garment of corruptibility and mortality, what is more important is that a garment of incorruptibility is put on. What is of interest for our concern in understanding this witness to the identity and mission of the baptized is that the Frankish Church did not tie the meaning to a dramatic clothing switch, as had earlier generations. Its focus was on the unction or chrismation as the significant act of vesting, for the garment being put on at baptism is nothing less than Christ and Christ's Holy Spirit.

Accompanying this ritual clothing with holy chrism was a verbal elaboration of what was occurring: this chrism put on as a garment was identified as the sevenfold gift of the Spirit, once proclaimed by the prophet Isaiah as the garment of the messianic king.[8] Yet even this allusion to Isaiah's messianic oracle was packed with a greater density of meaning than appears at first notice. Because ritual language is allusive, whoever wants to understand it must follow the many directions in which it points. The Gallican liturgies wove webs of meaning for this baptismal outfit of chrism on a loom stretched between Isaiah and Luke-Acts. The meaning is available, not through a strategy of human logic, but through the strategy that created it: openness to the Paraclete teaching the Church the way of salvation.

According to all the Gospels, when Jesus came up out of the water bath of the Jordan, the Holy Spirit enveloped or covered him (Luke 3:21-22). According to Luke's Gospel, when Jesus subsequently presented himself to his own people as the one with a God-given mission, he did so by citing the messianic oracle of Deutero-Isaiah: "The Spirit of the Lord is upon me. . . ." (61:1). That oracle concludes with lines not cited by Luke, but familiar in the Church: "Let me rejoice in the Lord with all my heart . . . for he has robed me in salvation as a garment and clothed me in integrity as a cloak" (61:10). Isaiah's garment of salvation is the Spirit of the Lord upon the one chosen.

But this is not the end. In this Gallican baptismal tradition, the web of meaning requires a shuttling from Luke to Isaiah and

back to Luke, then on to Acts, and back to the prophet Joel.
Luke's Gospel closes with a foreshadowing of what is to come in
Acts, on Pentecost. The risen Lord Jesus tells his disciples that
they are to wait in the city until they themselves are, like him,
clothed (*endysesthe*) with power from on high (24:49). Then, in
reporting on the events of Pentecost, Luke borrows from the
oracle of the prophet Joel to account for what has happened.
God says that in the last days, "Yes, I will cover over even my
slaves, both men and women, with a portion of my spirit" (Acts
2:18).[9]

This great web of meaning is gathered up into the ritual
transaction of the chrismation of the tribal folk of the Frankish
kingdom, the Huns and their newborn infants. The Church ex-
travagantly identifies their baptismal chrismation with the messianic garment of immortality.[10] By the Holy Spirit given to
them in the anointing, God is regenerating, rehabilitating, fitting
them to take up new life with all its consequences. But for what
did the Church believe they were being suited? The prayer continues to provide the testimony.

As we suggested earlier, the density of ritual meaning is such
that everything that needs to be played out cannot be celebrated
in a single moment. So we must expand the focus of the inquiry
into this *theologia prima*, the imaginative expression of baptismal faith. We will look backward to the Holy Thursday rite
for the consecration of the chrism itself, and forward to the Sunday after Easter, when the great baptismal celebration was
reaching its denouement.

Among the texts provided for Holy Thursday in one of the
Gallican liturgical books is the prayer for the consecration of
chrism, used also in the Roman Church to this day. It proclaims
that the chrism is to be used so that "they also may be made thy
Christs."[11] The prayer conceives of the chrism as a garment of
power, to be worn as a visible sacrament of the royal, priestly,
and prophetic honor that accrues to the baptized as bearers of
the name Christ. The formula actually establishes a ritual frame

of meaning for identifying the newly baptized. It is repeated in a prayer said on Easter day, after the baptisms have occurred. Having sketched Christ's messianic role as that of priest, prophet, and king, it notes that the baptized were incorporated into his life in order to share in his functions.[12]

When, on the Sunday after Easter, the *Clausum Paschae*, the newly baptized removed the material white garment of their baptism, they did so at the end of a liturgical rite that had once again proclaimed the text of Isaiah 61, "The Spirit of the Lord is upon me . . .," a text that had reverberated in overtones and undertones during all the baptismal events.[13] The newly baptized were confronted with a saving paradox: even though the Church directed them to set aside the outward white robe, they had all received an abiding garment of splendor — their anointing with the Spirit.

The Church of Charlemagne did not moderate its convictions about the power and purpose of baptism. Alcuin, advisor to Charlemagne, clearly believed that the baptized had been strengthened by the Holy Spirit for the purpose of preaching to others (*ad praedicandum aliis*) the faith they had received at baptism.[14] He saw in the unlikely *rudes*, to whom the Church was capable of giving only the most rudimentary presentation of the gospel, people who were by the design of God radically fit for a messianic mission. This was a Church whose poverty of resources was great. Its people were an illiterate and semi-literate folk, and their ordained leaders were much like them. It was a Church cut off from its Jewish and Hellenistic past and, as a result, incapable of offering its members a full formation in the gospel as a source of meaning. Yet the Church's liturgy continued to entertain the truth and keep alive the faith that all the baptized are, by God's deed, chosen and outfitted for the preaching of the gospel.

If we ask why this era maintained such a high doctrine of holy baptism when it was not in any way able to equip all the baptized for an actual exercise of a full Christian vocation, we must fall back on the essentially conservative character of the baptismal liturgy. It is a reliable witness to sound traditional faith, despite social conditions that obstructed its enfleshment.

Underneath the ritual entertainment of the root metaphor of messianic vesting lies the basis for the more abstract notion that the Church's sacramental activity *fits* the Church for its mission. If the magisterial and theological traditions from the high Middle Ages tie preaching to ordination on the grounds that the ordained have "a certain sacred fitness" for the task, it is necessary to critique whatever absolute claims are implicit in this argument. The unbroken witness of the baptismal liturgy, maintained even in one of its least favored epochs, asserts that the sacred fitness for joining in the messianic mission, and so in the preaching ministry that is part of it, is a gift given at baptism.

Cyril's Jerusalem. To appreciate the baptismal faith that the Church of Charlemagne was professing liturgically but was unable to conserve operationally, we can compare its witness with the doctrine and practice of Cyril and the Christian community within which he presided in the fourth century at Jerusalem. Cyril's episcopacy also occurred in an expansionist era. Christianity had been made legal and was about to be made obligatory for the citizens of the Roman Empire. But two witnesses to Cyril's milieu show an ecclesial life that was circumstantially different from the world about which Alcuin wrote to Charlemagne. Both the Jewish and Hellenistic cultures on which the Mediterranean Churches were built enjoyed longstanding and highly developed traditions of literacy and rhetorical skill able to be directed to the service of preaching the gospel.

The Spanish noblewoman-nun Egeria, traveling to Jerusalem in the midst of the excitement of its boom years, kept a journal that gives us an outsider's observations about the Eastern Mediterranean Church in operation in the fourth century. She reported that preaching was an important part of Jerusalem Church life, and so many were so eager to preach that the bishop allowed several presbyters to preach in turn in assemblies at which he presided.[15]

Eusebius, bishop of Caesarea by vocation and Church historian by avocation, reported an even fuller range of preaching practice in the generations before Cyril. He cites a letter to the emperor from two bishops (one of them a predecessor of Cyril) saying that they know of several situations in which the bishop has invited a lay person to preach and that they presume the practice is common. Eusebius the bishop-historian then notes that the practice of lay preaching is in no way forbidden but is in fact the way the famous Origen got his start as preacher "though not yet ordained to the presbyterate."[16]

What equipped the laity for this work? At a human level, perhaps human skills of interpretation and rhetoric. But Cyril was himself quite eloquent about the way in which baptism radically fitted the baptized for full participation in the messianic mission. Cyril wrote in his mystagogical catechesis "On the Holy Chrism": "[the anointing] shall teach you all things."[17] He specified that what the neophytes would learn from their anointing was that they were figures of Christ.[18] His approach to the transformation of the neophytes through the rites of initiation has been called mimesis theology.[19] It is a rich manifestation of *theologia prima*, the expressive and allusive testimony to living faith that precedes and exceeds its systematic thematization.

Cyril started with a text from 1 John (2:20-28) aimed to assure the baptized of the importance of their anointing: it is "real and no illusion." Then he elaborated: What happened to Jesus happens to the disciple. When Jesus came up out of the waters of the Jordan, the Spirit covered him, anointing him for his messianic mission. Such is the case with the neophyte.

But what is the messianic mission? Cyril recalled the Old Testament accounts of the anointing of priests and kings, but unlike the Frankish interpreters, not for the sake of comparison but for contrast.[20] Great as were the priests and kings, they shared neither in the gift of the Spirit of Jesus nor in his mission.

Cyril looked elsewhere for the meaning. He cited the Letter to the Ephesians (6:11-20), where they were exhorted to put on all the protective armor that God provides: the belt of truth, the coat of integrity, the shoes of the gospel of peace. Here his mimesis theology draws upon the clothing metaphor, which seems a constant in the tradition. For Cyril, the Ephesians text echoes the Isaiah text (11:5) that sings of the messianic heir who will be wearing around his waist the belt of justice and on his body the mail of good faith. The one so clothed can be recognized as the one on whom the Spirit of the Lord has come to rest, the spirit of wisdom and understanding, counsel and power, of knowledge and fear of the Lord (11:2).

Cyril gathers these texts to point to the meaning: Just as Jesus' anointing was for the mission of the gospel of peace, so is the anointing that accompanies the water bath a messianic commissioning by the power of the Holy Spirit. For Cyril, these ideas are neither abstract theories, nor religious gnosis, nor mystical or vaguely futuristic in their reference. They are also operational. The neophyte is actually empowered to cooperate in the messianic work: "He hath anointed me to preach glad tidings to the poor."[21]

To underscore this point of messianic transformation, Cyril continues to focus on the anointing, even as he engages another metaphor, defying the conventions of logic. The anointing on the forehead is not only an outfitting for the messianic mission; it is also an unveiling.[22] Cyril recalls Paul's teaching that the baptized "with uncovered faces . . . reflect as in a mirror the glory of God" (2 Cor 3:18). The shining splendor of the oiled countenance was for Paul a manifestation of the restoration of humankind to God's image, a work of the Holy Spirit of Jesus. By association, the baptized and anointed neophytes mirror forth the glory of God with their shining foreheads. The mimetic significance is then underscored. "You are Christs," he says unqualifiedly to his assembly.[23] Just as Christ, the anointed, the perfect image of the Father, was the One sent as a messenger, so the anointed Christian, in his image, is also a messenger of the good news.

A full plumbing not only of Cyril but of the whole liturgical tradition of the early centuries would yield a vast list of citations woven together into fabrics of meaning, some intricate, some elaborate, some homespun. Why cite them at all? They serve to put into perspective the theological tradition that uses the language of empowerment by the Holy Spirit, a certain sacred fitness, and the sacramental imaging of Christ as technical language that has the ordained clergy as its primary referent.[24] That tradition has the whole thing backward. If the witness of the *theologia prima* is given credence, if the norm for believing is in some authentic way tied to the norm of the Church's public prayer, then things commonly claimed for the ordained as the basis for preaching are already attributable to every person growing into the fullness of the one baptismal gift of the Spirit with its many charismatic manifestations.

Systematizing and Narrowing the Tradition

The Church celebrated the same faith in its eighth-century poverty as in its fourth-century abundance. Nevertheless, the witness of the baptismal liturgy was set aside by the twelfth century for many reasons. One important one was the rise of a novel conceptual scheme among practitioners of *theologia secunda*, the systematic theology of the schools. As a result of this development, ordination underwent a pseudo-sacralization and baptism was profaned.[25] The circumstances of the second Christian millennium encouraged these developments.

The preaching of the gospel had deteriorated during the early medieval period, as Alcuin testified. Although the Church grew numerically, it no longer had access to the knowledge nor possessed the skill necessary to preach in the rabbinic tradition of a Paul, nor did it have many trained in the classical rhetorical tradition familiar to an Origen or Augustine. Councils enjoined bishops to see to it that pastors formed those they had baptized with the living word of the gospel. But bishops often settled for compromise, encouraging the use of Latin sermon texts from earlier generations to be read, where possible, by the pastors to the people.[26] That strategy filled the breach. But the mystery of the baptized Christian as a living image of Christ outfitted for the messianic mission was celebrated during the eighth through the twelfth centuries primarily in faithfulness to the received tradition rather than as a lively truth.

Monastic scriptoria prepared for the eventual rise of the theological schools of the high Middle Ages; the schools stimulated new interest in organizing and interpreting the faith of the Church. Reform movements invigorated ecclesial life. By the twelfth century, interest in preaching the gospel and the requisite literacy, grammatical competence, and rhetorical skills had revived. As a result, for several generations preaching was "out of control" in a Church unprepared to order the resurgence of the charism of preaching. Lay preaching had erupted, had been sanctioned, subject to episcopal or papal approval, and had been suppressed in the wake of clerical objections. The acts of synods and councils document the problem.[27]

Thomas Aquinas, writing in the thirteenth century, reflects the tensions that several generations of new experiences of preaching had spawned.[28] Is preaching properly limited only to those priest-pastors to whom the bishop has given the care of souls? Is it fitting to have a religious order of preachers? Is it fitting that preachers should live on the alms of the people? Can monks preach to the world if they have died to the world? Thomas's writings also reflect a significant theological development that would effectively weaken the witness of the baptismal liturgy, even though that liturgy continued to celebrate the unbroken faith in the fitness of the baptized for an active role in the messianic mission. For via the Abbey of St. Victor in the eleventh century, the theologians of the medieval schools had become familiar with the conceptual scheme of a pseudonymous sixth-century work from Asia Minor, *The Ecclesiastical Hierarchies.*

This work, authored by one calling himself Dionysius — by inference, the companion of Paul the Apostle — provided systematicians with an influential logical schema derived from Hellenistic philosophy, namely, a distinction between active powers and passive powers.[29] Using this distinction, it was possible to affirm simultaneously and without apparent contradiction the notions that both the baptized and the ordained had a share in the gift of the Holy Spirit, but that the shares were qualitatively different. The laity's share was passive, the ordained's active. With their passive share, the laity could receive the other sacraments, hear the Word of God, receive the goods of salvation. With their active share, the ordained could confect sacraments, especially the Eucharist, and preach the gospel. The ordained were agents of the apostolic mission; the baptized were the recipients of the active work of the clergy. Systematic sacramental theology and ecclesiology and magisterial teaching have been frozen within this construct to this day.

In the revised rites of Vatican II, which are for the most part authentic witnesses to the ancient faith, we have a striking example of the power of this twelfth-century theological opinion to continue to assert itself and so to influence Church life, Church order, and consequently the theological reflection on the preaching ministry. What is ironic in that the encroachment of this construct on the baptismal liturgy has occurred so belatedly, and during this time of Church renewal.

The Chrism Mass of Holy Thursday has been, since the fifth century, a constant witness to the baptismal faith of the Roman Catholic Church. The consecratory prayer from the Gelasian Sacramentary exalts the chrism as solemnly if not as lavishly as the *Exsultet* of a later era praises the Easter candle during the Paschal Vigil. The prayer sings of the joy that the oil of the olive has brought to the world from the time that the dove brought the olive branch as a token of reconciliation and peace to Noah and his family. The prayer credits David the prophet with dubbing the chrism "oil of gladness" because God faithfully showed saving power through the anointing of priests, prophets, and kings.[30]

In its liturgical telling at the Chrism Mass, the story of the oil culminates in the account of the baptism of Jesus, on whom also the Spirit descended as a dove, a messenger to him of his messianic mission of peace. Then it focuses on the present: May those who will share the same anointing through the oil receive its power and so cooperate with Christ's messianic work. At the time of the origins of the great song of the chrism, the references were unambiguously baptismal, for the chrism was used exclusively for the baptized in the Roman liturgy. In fact, several centuries elapsed before Roman ordination rites incorporated actual ritual anointings of presbyters (and then their hands, not their heads) and before the hierarchy took up anointing kings and emperors.[31] These developments were secondary and derivative, and betrayed a reductionist reading of ancient baptismal texts, assuming them to refer to the actual social and ecclesiastical order, which by that time had no small number of priests and kings.

This ancient consecratory hymn is kept in the 1970 revised order of the Chrism Mass. Its ancient baptismal meaning echoes in the readings from Isaiah and Luke assigned for the celebration: "The Spirit has anointed me . . . to bring good news to the poor. . . ." But the baptismal intent is upstaged by an unprecedented development that makes this celebration of baptismal identity a minor theme in the revised Chrism Mass. The Roman Pontifical of 1970, breaking with the tradition, presents as a major motif of the Chrism Mass the celebration of the cultic priesthood shared by the ordained, bishops and their presbyters.[32]

However unwitting, the development is a bit of liturgical piracy — raiding the ship's hold for valuable cargo. On the basis of an examination of a new combination of texts, it can be shown that this liturgy intends to guarantee agency to the active and to encourage the laity to assent that their baptism is a deputation to dependence. The vocables "priest" and "priesthood" cannot ever entirely lose their rich baptismal meaning. But the 1970 rite fairly effectively narrows the reference in the Chrism Mass to the company of the ordained.[33] In this whole development from the twelfth to the twentieth centuries, the most high-handed act of encroachment of an ideology of ordained priesthood on the baptismal liturgy may be the composition, in this era, of a special preface of ordained priesthood to replace the ancient preface for this day, which had proclaimed the royal, priestly, and prophetic identity of the baptized.[34]

Where the Burden of Theological Argument Lies

The intent of this examination of the liturgical tradition of baptism has been to establish that first theology *(theologia prima)* knows more about the identity and ministerial vocation of the baptized than is reflected in the tradition of systematic theology *(theologia secunda)* since the Middle Ages. Church discipline more accurately reflects what the liturgy of baptism celebrates than systematic theology does. Church discipline has regularly provided for episcopal authorization of lay people as ministers of the Word in a wide range of situations. The discipline has at times strained the minds, hearts, and theological imaginations of those who have considered as divine law the Scholastic distinction between active and passive shares in the gift of the Holy Spirit. Given those foundations, theologians were forced to speculate on how the bishops effectively empowered the radically unsuited before commissioning them to preach.

At the present time the Church has good reason to rejoice in the living tradition that the non-ordained are fitted by baptism to be collaborators in the ministry of the Word as evangelists and catechists, as teachers and preachers. The 1973 indult to the West German bishops from the Congregation for the Clergy asserted that the non-ordained are even suited to give the liturgical homily upon proper episcopal authorization — an authorization a bishop also gives to presbyters.[35] Despite that document, a line of resistance persists in the theological community and in the magisterium which wishes to argue on theological grounds that the liturgical homily must be reserved to the ordained, or at least that this is the case with the Eucharistic homily. One of the most cogent presentations of that position is found in a 1965 essay by the eminent French liturgist Joseph Gelineau.[36]

Gelineau's reasoning deserves scrutiny, since his is a representative presentation of the most cogent rationale for what is commonly thought and taught to be the Church's official position, the 1973 letter of the Congregation for the Clergy to the contrary notwithstanding. According to Gelineau, it is ordination that fits the ordained minister for the public celebration of the mystery of the Word of God. The homily is, by definition, that form of public commentary on Scripture suited to bishop, presbyter, and deacon because of the hierarchical status conferred by their ordination.[37] (Gelineau's phrase "apanage de l'evêque" means literally that the bishop has the bread, metaphorically, that he is equipped for exercising his role in life. Note: we are back to a variation on the clothing metaphor.) But at this point the argument is circular. Furthermore, it reflects dual assumptions: (1) that the merely baptized are unsuited for the public ministry of the Word because the Holy Spirit is a passive presence within them, and (2) that the Holy Spirit is activated by ordination.

The theological argument for reserving the liturgical homily to the ordained seems to be suspended over an abyss created by the unexamined Scholastic distinction between active and passive endowments of the Spirit of Christ. Nevertheless, Gelineau's concern for the finality of the liturgical homily is on more solid ground. He conceives of the homilist as exercising a ministry of mediation, as guiding the assembly of believers into communion with the mystery of salvation-present that is being celebrated. Mediation is by definition a priestly function. But it remains unclear on what legitimate grounds it can be maintained that the priestly, royal, and prophetic identity and mission of the baptized leaves them radically unsuited for this mediatorial task. To assert as much is to profane Christian baptism, a condition toward which the tradition of systematic sacramental theology has been contributing wittingly and unwittingly for too many centuries.

In all of this, there is no intention to negate the necessity of an orderly Church nor to deny episcopal responsibility for ordering the exercise of the ministry of the Word, whether the preachers have received holy baptism or both holy baptism and holy orders. But the hard fact is that the Church does not have a systematic sacramental theology adequate to the data of ecclesial life past or present. Least of all does the Roman Catholic Church have an adequate systematic theology of baptism, perhaps because of a hypertrophic interest in ordination.[38] Baptismal theology has been preoccupied with the notion of the removal of original sin, on the one hand, and with the effort, on the other, to advance the odd position that Christians whom God has chosen to empower for the messianic mission nevertheless remain pneumatic cripples in the Church.

The question of the tie between Word and Sacrament, especially but not exclusively in the Eucharist, remains. But theologians must seek a theological model for understanding someplace other than in past theories of sacramentality that too quickly identify the ordained with the image of Christ in such a way that he is exclusively *in persona Christi* for the rest of the Church. The baptismal liturgy, confirmed by postconciliar ecclesial experience, suggests that sacramentality is a quality of the whole *ecclesia*, the community of those who are being transformed slowly, by God's power, into living images of the saving Christ. It is the whole Church together that makes Eucharist, says the new experience, although the Church struggles with the residual question of whether the one who prays the prayer and says the words of institution is not the one who really counts after all.

But if the Eucharist is the act of the whole Church, and if the ordained is someone who presides within, not over, the community of believers, then it seems both possible and necessary to seek new models for understanding sacramentality in relationship to liturgical presidency. Ecclesial experience confirms that it is possible for the one who presides within the liturgical assembly by office to engage another believer to lead them all together into deeper communion with the mystery of Christ by the power of the Word, and that this collaborative ordering does not fracture the sacrament of unity. Perhaps the question is whether the presidency of the ordained minister in the liturgical assembly inevitably involves prelacy or may just as authentically manifest collaboration within the one Body.

Unless and until the theology of baptism and the theology of ordination are examined together within the theological community for their christological and pneumatological foundations and for their adequacy to contemporary Christian experience, those who want to find solid ground for developing lay collaboration in the full preaching ministry, including liturgical preaching, will be kept on the defensive. But the witness of the baptismal liturgy shows convincingly that the burden of proof should rest rather with those who want to disqualify the laity as a class from preaching in any or all of its forms.

NOTES

1. R. T. Hanley, "The Theology of Preaching in Modern Papal Teaching," Catholic University of America Dissertation Series 2, no. 155 (1964) 52.

2. *Ibid.*, 57.

3. Session VII, On the Sacraments, canon 10; see H. Denzinger-A. Schönmetzer, *Enchiridion symbolorum definitionum et declarationum de rebus fidei et morum*, 36th ed. (Rome: Herder, 1976) 1610.

4. Eusebius, *History of the Church*, trans. G. A. Williamson (Baltimore: Penguin Books, 1965) 260 [6:19].

5. Hanley, "Theology of Preaching," 49–52.

6. Alcuin to Charlemagne, *Monumenta Germaniae Historica: Epistolae Carolini Aevi*, ed. E. Dümmler, Series 18, tome IV, letter 110.

7. A. Chavasse, "La bénédiction du chrême en Gaule avant l'adoption intégrale de la liturgie romaine," *Revue du moyen-âge latin* 1 (1945) 111–113. See, for example, *Missale Gothicum*, Henry Bradshaw Society 52, ed. H. M. Bannister (London, 1917). For a discussion, see J. Levesque, "The Theology of the Postbaptismal Rites in the Gallican Liturgical Sources of the Seventh and Eighth Centuries," Catholic University of America Dissertation Series 2, no. 266 (1977).

8. *The Gregorian Sacramentary*, Henry Bradshaw Society 49, ed. H. A. Wilson (London, 1915): Oratio ad infantes consignandos, pp. 57–58; also *Liber sacramentorum Romae Aeclesiae Ordinis anni circuli* [Gelasian Sacramentary], Sacramentorum Cod. Vat. Reg. Lat. 316, ed. C. Mohlberg (Rome: Herder, 1968) no. 451. Parallels also in the sacramentaries of Gellone (no. 711) and Angoulême (no. 761).

9. "Legenda in Sancto Pentecosten," *Le lectionnaire de Luxeuil*, Collectanea Biblica Latina 7, ed. P. Salmon (Rome, 1944–53) 1:173–175.

10. Levesque, "Theology of the Postbaptismal Rites," 43–49. See *Missale Gothicum*, no. 261; there are echoes also in the Holy Thursday chrism preface of the Gelasian Sacramentary.

11. *Missale Gallicanum Vetus*, Chrism Mass, "Contestatio," no. 82. Translation from L. Mitchell in *Baptismal Anointing*, Alcuin Club Collections 48 (London: SPCK, 1966) 118. For a discussion of this, see Levesque, "Theology of the Postbaptismal Rites," 95ff.

12. See Levesque, "Theology of the Postbaptismal Rites," 96–101, 107–108; also *Missale Gallicanum Vetus*, no. 195.

13. "Legenda clausum Paschae," *Le lectionnaire de Luxeuil*, 1:133.

14. Alcuin to Oduin, *Monumenta Germaniae Historica: Epistolae Carolini Aevi*, ed. E. Dümmler, Series 18, tome IV, letter 134. See also Levesque, "Theology of the Postbaptismal Rites," 175. The meaning of

praedicandum in medieval Latin has been disputed. C. Mohrmann shows that in the course of the fourth century the verb *praedicare*, used in earlier generations to designate the preaching of the Lord and the apostles, came to mean preaching done in the Church. Even when ecclesial circumstances curtailed that "preaching" to reading texts, the language was not entirely cut off from its original matrix. See "Praedicare, Tractare, Sermo: Essai sur la terminologie de la prédication paleochrétienne," *La Maison-Dieu* 39 (1954) 101ff. For an illustration of the medieval equation of "preaching" with reading of texts, see Peter Lombard, *IV Sentences*, dist. 24, cap. vi, on the office of reader.

15. *Egeria's Travels*, trans. J. Wilkinson (London: SPCK, 1971) 125 [25:1].

16. Eusebius, *History of the Church*, 260 [6:19].

17. *St. Cyril of Jerusalem's Lectures on the Christian Sacraments*, ed. F. L. Cross (London: SPCK, 1951): "On the Holy Chrism," 3:7, 66.

18. *Ibid.*, 3:1, 64.

19. H. Riley, *Christian Initiation*, Studies in Christian Antiquity 17, ed. J. Quasten (Washington: University Press of America) 365–367.

20. *Ibid.*, 368.

21. *St. Cyril of Jerusalem's Lectures*, 3:1, 64. For an extended theological reflection on Cyril's teaching, see Riley, *Christian Initiation*, 365–379.

22. *St. Cyril of Jerusalem's Lectures*, 3:4, 65. See also Riley, *Christian Initiation*, 372–373.

23. *St. Cyril of Jerusalem's Lectures*, 3:1, 64.

24. See, for example, the appropriation of this baptismal witness to serve purposes of clerical self-definition in Peter Lombard, *IV Sentences*, dist. 24, cap. iii: "Tales enim decet esse ministros Christi qui septiformi gratia Spiritus sancti sint decori. . . . In sacramento ergo septiformis Spiritus septem sunt gradus ecclesiastici. . . ." Also, in cap. iv: "Unde ministri Ecclesiae reges esse debent, ut se et alios regant; quibus Petrus ait [1 Pet 2:9]: 'Vos estis genus electum, regale sacerdotium,'" found in the context of interpreting the clerical tonsure.

25. M. Collins, "The Public Language of Ministry," *The Jurist* 41 (December, 1981) 261–294.

26. For an account of these developments, see H. Dressler, "Preaching (History of)," *New Catholic Encyclopedia* (New York: McGraw-Hill, 1967); also E. C. Dargan, *A History of Preaching* (New York: Armstrong, 1905) 132–137 and *passim*.

27. For an account of the Waldensians and the Humiliati, see L. Christiani, "Vaudois," *Dictionnaire de théologie catholique* 15/2; also F. Vernet, "Humiliés," *Dictionnaire de théologie catholique* 7/1.

28. *Summa theologiae,* II-II, 183-189; see *The Pastoral and Religious Lives,* Summa Theologiae Series 47 (New York: McGraw-Hill, 1964).

29. For these ideas in Aquinas, see *Summa theologiae,* III, 62-72, and especially 63, 6, in *Baptism and Confirmation,* Summa Theologiae Series 57 (New York: McGraw-Hill, 1964): "Sed ad agentes in sacramentis pertinet sacramentum ordinis . . . ad recipientes pertinet sacramentum baptismi." Interestingly, however, Aquinas cites a text from Rabanus Maurus, itself a citation of his mentor Alcuin (see note 14 above), as an objection to the details of this logical schema, and responds that God is not bound by the sacraments(!): "virtus divina non est alligata sacramentis" (III, 72, 6). See also G. Thery, "L'entrée du Ps-Denys en Occident," *Mélanges Mandonnet,* Bibliothèque thomiste 14 (Paris: J. Vrin, 1930) 2:23-30; *Dionysius the Pseudo-Areopagite: The Ecclesiastical Hierarchies,* ed. T. Campbell (Washington: University Press of America, 1981).

30. *The Rites of the Catholic Church* (New York: Pueblo Publishing Co., 1980) 1:303. For a full discussion of the origins and history of this text, see H. Schmidt, *Hebdomada Sancta,* 3 vols. (Rome: Herder, 1957).

31. D. Power, *Ministers of Christ and His Church* (London: G. Chapman, 1969) 89-93 and 193, on the appropriation of both the anointing and the vesting metaphors.

32. "Ordo benedicendi oleum catechumenorum et infirmorum et conficiendi chrisma," *Pontificale Romanum* (Vatican City: Typis Polyglottis Vaticanis, 1971) Praenotanda 1.

33. F. Henderson, "The Chrism Mass of Holy Thursday," *Worship* 51 (1977) 149-158.

34. For the priesthood preface, see the 1970 Roman Missal; for the earlier preface, which is found in Pius XII's restored order of Holy Week, see *Ordo Hebdomadae Sanctae instauratur* (Vatican City: Typis Polyglottis Vaticanis, 1956) or Schmidt, *Hebdomada Sancta* 1:65.

35. Letter of John Cardinal Wright, prefect of the Sacred Congregation for the Clergy, to Julius Cardinal Doepfner, president of the Episcopal Conference of West Germany (November 20, 1973) 4; also, Decree on Lay Preaching, Roman Catholic Synod of West Germany, 2:32-2:34; see *Canon Law Digest* 8 (1973-77) 941-944.

36. J. Gelineau, "L'homélie, Forme plénière de la prédication," *La Maison-Dieu* 82 (1965) 29-42.

37. *Ibid.,* 34.

38. Even the excellent introduction to liturgy, *L'Église en prière,* ed. A. G. Martimort, 3rd ed. (Paris: Desclée, 1965) gives a logical and theological priority to ordination over baptism. See also Martimort, *The Signs of the New Covenant* (Collegeville, Minn.: The Liturgical Press, 1963).

Lay Preaching and Canon Law in a Time of Transition

The theological dimensions of this topic have already been addressed. My task is to explore the provisions of Church law relative to preaching by the non-ordained.

Let me first make a preliminary remark on method. There are three approaches to a study such as this from a canon law point of view. The first is theoretical, exploring the theological foundations for law and the ideal ordering of Church life. This approach would present what *ought to be the law*. The second is expository, presenting the provisions of the current law of the Church. This approach would explain what *is to be done* in the present order, the standards which are now to be observed even if they have not always been this way, and which could change in the future. The third approach is exegetical, analyzing the law in text and context, and asking what is possible even under historically conditioned, limited provisions of the law. This presents what *can be done*, taking advantage of all the exceptions built into the law as it stands.

Studies on theology have presented much of what ought to be. I suspect that most readers are fairly well acquainted with current standards. So the approach in this study will explore what can be done, using a traditional conservative legal exegesis.

A second preliminary comment on Church law, the raw material for this study, may also be helpful. Church law is like a skeleton that gives structural frame and form to the body. While it is the basis for the strength and power in a body, it can also inhibit a body's movements. So, too, law can inhibit the response of the Body of Christ, the Church, to the impulses of the Spirit. Law, therefore, must be interpreted carefully, adapted appropriately, and renewed or revised regularly.

Pope John XXIII recognized this need and called for an "aggiornamento" of the 1917 Code of Canon Law at the same time that he called for a pastoral, ecumenical council.[1] Since Vatican II, work has progressed in revising the Code. But we have also come to experience since the Council the fact that Church law is broader than the Code. A renewed way of looking at the Church gives us new insight into the workings of law within the Church.[2]

The sources of Church law today include the 1917 Code, the documents of the Second Vatican Council, postconciliar decrees that look to implementing the Council and the renewal that carries its name. Church law is also found in liturgical law, chiefly the norms at the beginning of the various rituals; it exists in particular law, in special indults or permissions given to various parts of the Church, and in the customs of Church people.[3]

The revised Code has finally been promulgated, and I am going to deal with it rather extensively to set the perspective in which the Church's law is moving, and also to provide some idea of what the future will hold.[4] I want to begin with some theoretical reflections on the basic framework in which the law, old and revised, deals with preaching. Then I will examine certain forms of preaching and the role of lay people in their regard. Finally, I will make a few comments looking toward the future.

I. The Basic Legal Framework

In the 1917 Code of Canon Law, preaching is part of the work of magisterium. Magisterium itself is an exercise of jurisdiction.[5] It pertains to the hierarchy of jurisdiction, headed by the pope and bishops, and participated in by those whom they call to their aid. This view of teaching or preaching is rooted in the more fundamental concept that the Church is *societas inaequalis*, a society of at least two classes — those who govern, and those they rule.[6] Applied to the area of magisterium, there is the *ecclesia docens*, the "teaching Church," and the *ecclesia discens*, the "learning Church."[7]

In the Code, the first category of magisterium is preaching the divine Word. Under it, canons on catechetics come first; then, norms about sermons given during or outside the liturgy, but primarily in the church building. These are followed by rules governing seminaries, schools, the censure of books, and the profession of faith.[8]

As I mentioned, preaching as well as other exercises of this magisterium belong fundamentally to the pope and bishops, and to those they choose to associate with themselves in this work. Lay people are excluded from preaching in church, something that is considered an exercise of jurisdictional power.[9]

Vatican II introduced into official Church teaching a new way of thinking. In place of the *societas inaequalis* of the 1917 Code, the Church appears as the community of the baptized, who are equal in the dignity and activity that are theirs by virtue of baptism.[10] Preaching is not a governmental activity but an exercise of the *munus docendi** — the teaching mission of Christ himself, committed to the Church to be carried out in Christ's name until the end of time.[11]

Baptism gives a basic participation in the *munera* of Christ.[12] A different participation in those *munera* comes through the sacrament of orders, which gives the ordained, not a "super-Christian" or more perfect participation, but a different kind of

---

*The Latin term *munus* used by Vatican Council II to refer to a function, service, office, or other responsibility, can be translated in several ways, but it is generally used in a fairly broad sense to refer to various dimensions of the Church's mission, such as the teaching *munus*, sanctifying *munus*, and the *munus* of government.

participation in Christ's *munera*.[13] Ordination does not exclude what comes from baptism but provides the basis for ordering it in the communion and mission of the Church itself.[14]

The revised Code attempts to reflect this new way of thinking.[15] A whole book is devoted to the *munus docendi*, rather than relegating this to a section of the treatment on "things" as found in the 1917 Code. It is a *munus* in which all in the Church participate by virtue of baptism, and for which various persons have different responsibilities in virtue of their functions in the Church.

This book on the *munus docendi* is organized under five titles or sections: the ministry of the divine Word, the missionary work of the Church, Catholic education, the media of social communications, and the profession of faith.[16] Some of this is left over from the old Code; much of it is new, reflecting the Council's teaching and the changed circumstances of the Church today. This organization also reflects the basic position that the *munus docendi* is done by preaching, by catechetical instruction, by teaching, and through public declarations issued in the name of the Church by proper authorities.[17]

Preaching as such is considered under the broader rubric of the "ministry of the divine Word." The title may be the same, but the understanding of what is involved in the ministry of the divine Word has undergone an evolution since the 1917 Code. This ministry is now presented as the *munus evangelii annuntiandi*—the *munus* of announcing the gospel to the world and in the Church.[18] In the perspective of Pope Paul VI, evangelization has many dimensions, not only the proclaiming of the gospel to those who have not yet heard it or been baptized.[19] This same perspective continues in the revised Code. This ministry of the Word must be nourished by Scripture, tradition, liturgy, the magisterium and life of the Church. The mystery of Christ, the canon continues, must be expressed integrally and faithfully by those who carry out this ministry.[20]

Announcing the gospel is a special responsibility of the pope and the college of bishops, and of bishops individually. Presbyters and deacons have a special role as well, as do religious and lay persons.[21] Religious and lay people, in addition to their own proper role in the ministry of the Word, can also be invited to assist the bishops and presbyters in their work.[22]

Reversing the order of the 1917 Code, the revised text considers preaching (and not just "sermons") before it deals with catechetical instruction. Bishops have a right (ius) to preach everywhere.[23] Presbyters and deacons, upon ordination, have the faculty (facultas) to preach provided at least that they have the presumed permission of the rector of the church. This universal preaching faculty can be restricted, however, by their bishops or by particular law.[24] But the intent is to emphasize the conciliar teaching that the first duty of sacred ministers is to preach the gospel.[25]

Lay people under the revised Code can be admitted to preaching in church buildings (note the near play on words — preaching in church when church building is meant). This can be due to the needs of the situation or because it would be useful. The bishops' conference can set down norms about lay preaching, and there is a restriction with regard to the homily, which I will address later.[26]

The understanding of preaching proposed in the revised Code is interesting. One canon states that preachers are first to propose to the faithful what they are to believe and do for the glory of God and the salvation of human persons. They also are to impart the doctrine that the magisterium proposes concerning the dignity and freedom of the human person, the unity and stability of the family and its functions, the obligations that pertain to each in relation to others in society, and the proper ordering of this world's goods according to God's will.[27] All this is to be done in a manner adapted to the conditions of the hearers and the needs of the times.[28]

Bishops may issue norms concerning preaching in their dioceses and can require various kinds of preaching, such as

every Christian gives through the examp...
the words by which each gives an explan...
is in us.[35] It is preaching in the name of th...
within the church building itself, that re...

Traditional norms in Church law p...
receive the required authorization either...
held or through special delegation someti...
For example, the office of pastor incl...
responsibility to supervise the proces...
Rite of Christian Initiation of Adults), to...
supplied in the parish on various occasi...
homilies are provided at Masses on appro...
this came with his office rather than throu...
bishop.[37]

To preach in a diocese, a presbyter (w...
there) or a deacon had to receive permissio...
dinary.[38] This usually came in the form of "...
which were a concession by the bishop rathe...
individual. As mentioned earlier, the revise...
situation. It is now presumed that with ordi...
presbyter has the faculty to preach unless h...
stricted.[39] Nevertheless, the fact of ordinatio...
zation to perform those duties required of th...
effect, the revised Code continues the princip...
but with a remarkable flexibility.

For other persons to preach, authorizatio...
general, the prohibition against lay persons p...
continued all the way up to the revised Cod...
some notable exceptions in later Church law.

A. PREACHING BY LAY PERSONS IN GENERAL

The Rite of Christian Initiation of Adults c...
community to be involved in the process of...
catechizing. The catechesis is provided by a va...
lay as well as deacons and priests. In particular...

given a prominent role, perhaps one of the most significant forms of preaching by lay persons, since the catechist is the one who provides the basic foundation for the candidate's understanding and practice of the faith.[41]

Of course, this is not new. While the 1917 Code called for pastors to provide catechetical instruction personally, it did permit them to associate others — clergy, religious, or lay persons — with themselves in the work of catechesis.[42] In practice, the exception became the rule, and the living magisterium which has provided the basic formation in faith for bishops, clergy, and most of the Church has actually come from religious and lay persons who staffed schools or conducted religious education programs.[43]

What is new is the official recognition given to this function in the rite and the liturgical as well as practical importance placed on the role of the catechist in the various rites of the initiation process. Another exception is the instruction given by lectors, whether instituted by the bishop permanently in this ministry or exercising it on a less permanent basis. They are to "instruct the faithful for the worthy reception of the sacraments," an activity that may take place in the church.[44] Lay leaders or commentators may make various comments within the liturgy, avoiding exaggeration and limiting themselves to what is necessary.[45] With permission of the local ordinary, lay persons at sacred celebrations of the Word may witness to their lives, lead a meditation, engage in a dialogue, or read a homily indicated by the bishop or pastor.[46] Likewise, with the local ordinary's permission, lay persons such as catechists may be deputed to conduct the Liturgy of the Word when there is a shortage of priests.[47]

Although priests or deacons are the ordinary ministers for the exposition of the Eucharist, in their absence a lay person — acolyte, special minister of communion, religious or lay man or woman — may be appointed to expose and repose the Eucharist. During such exposition there should be readings from Scripture

with a homily or brief exhortation to develop a better understanding of the Eucharistic mystery.[48] Similarly, at Masses with
young children, adults, with the permission of the pastor or rector, may address the children after the gospel, particularly if the
priest has difficulty in adapting himself to the children's frame of
mind.[49]

In effect, then, the current law of the Church admits of a
number of exceptions to the previous norm that all lay persons,
including religious, are prohibited from preaching in church.
The revised Code completes this evolution by stating just the opposite of the 1917 norm, namely, that lay persons may preach in
a church or oratory if the circumstances require it or if it seems
useful, and provided that the norms of the episcopal conference
are observed. The one exception is the homily.[50] Because the
homily is excluded from lay preaching in principle, let us now
analyze what is involved in this form of preaching from the
standpoint of canon law.

B. THE HOMILY AND LAY PREACHING

1. Definition of homily

The First Instruction for the Proper Implementation of the
Constitution on the Liturgy gives what has become the standard
definition of a homily: "By a homily from the sacred text is
understood an explanation either of some aspect of the readings
from holy Scripture or of another text from the Ordinary or
Proper of the Mass of the day, taking into account the mystery
which is being celebrated and the particular needs of the
hearers."[51] By it, "the mysteries of the faith and the guiding principles of the Christian life are expounded from the sacred text
during the course of the liturgical year."[52] It is an integral part of
the liturgy.[53] These definitions are taken up in the revised introduction to the Lectionary, and form the basis for the definition of a homily proposed in the revised Code.[54]

It should be noted that a homily is not restricted to the
liturgy of the celebration of the Eucharist. It also appears in

various other liturgical rites, for example: in the various stages of the initiation of adults; for confirmation, even when administered outside Mass; at penance services; when Communion is distributed outside Mass; for funerals when there is no Eucharist; and so on.[55] The normal presumption is that these celebrations are conducted by lay persons, and for several of these rites explicit provision is made for the replacement of the homily by a meditation, instruction, or even the reading of a homily approved by the pastor. The focus of our concern, therefore, will be on the homily during the celebration of the Eucharist, as this is the key restriction on lay preaching today.

2. Minister of the homily

It is appropriate to distinguish the ordinary minister of the homily from the extraordinary minister.[56] We have become accustomed to this distinction in other liturgical practices, from baptism to distribution of the Eucharist.[57] The distinction, however, has a special canonical meaning that is not always obvious from the usual meaning of the word "ordinary."

Canonically, the term "ordinary" refers to a function that comes with an office.[58] It is something a person is entitled to do, even required to do, in virtue of the office or function the person holds in the Church. An extraordinary minister is one who does not have that designated, permanent role but nevertheless provides the service or function. For example, the lay ministry of lector may be exercised by one who is installed permanently in that ministry. The lector is thus the ordinary minister of the reading of the Word. If the celebrating priest or a deacon reads the readings before the gospel, he is acting as an "extraordinary minister" in that celebration, replacing the one who properly should do it. Interestingly, the revised introduction to the Lectionary states that "the liturgical assembly truly requires readers, even those not instituted. Proper measures must therefore be taken to ensure that there are qualified lay persons who have been trained to carry out this ministry."[59]

Who is the ordinary minister of the homily? The General Instruction of the Roman Missal states that "the homily should ordinarily be given by the celebrant."[60] On January 11, 1971, the Pontifical Commission for the Interpretation of the Decrees of the Second Vatican Council gave a negative reply to an inquiry that asked whether this norm, because of the use of the term "ordinarily," could be interpreted to mean that others, men and women, may give the homily.[61] The reply, however, seems to have been misleading, for immediately afterward an authoritative interpretation of the response was given by V. Carbone, moderator of the archives of the Second Vatican Council, disclaiming that it was intended to address the question of whether sometimes, for a reasonable cause, the liturgical homily could be committed to lay persons. The response was only meant to distinguish the celebrant from other clerics participating in the liturgy.[62]

Clearly, the office to which the *ordinary minister* of the homily is related is that of liturgical presidency. But there is another office involved as well — that of pastoral ministry. J. Frank Henderson makes a cogent argument for this in his recent study in *Worship*. "One of the most important requirements for effective preaching," he notes, "is one's relationship to the congregation."[63] This is usually assured through pastoral office.

Henderson identifies three characteristics of the ordinary minister of the homily. These are that the person be "[1] the ordained liturgical presider at the Eucharist, [2] who at the same time is a local pastor (that is, engaged in daily pastoral ministry to those preached to), and [3] who has devoted an appropriate amount of time, effort, thought, and prayer to preparation."[64] He also asserts the need for the proper gift to preach — not only that the person have the talent to preach but that preaching be the product of one's whole person.[65]

One could draw several implications from these characteristics, but let me single out only one. The ordinary minister of the homily is one who is authorized to preach in the name of the

Church. This is a traditional concept, but it is receiving a renewed meaning today. The Church in whose name one speaks is not just the hierarchical organization, although clearly those who are placed as pastors in the Church are responsible for good order in determining who does speak in the Church's name. But the Church is more than its officers; it is the people of God. Henderson argues that to speak "'in the name of' should no longer be viewed simply in terms of legal authorization by the bishop, but rather as a relationship of trust, responsibility and accountability with the whole Church, including the bishop but also the local congregation which the minister serves."[66]

Extraordinary ministers of the homily include presbyters who are not the liturgical presider at the Eucharist, or, if they are, who do not exercise a pastoral office on behalf of that community. Clearly, whoever delivers the homily must have an appropriate preparation and gift to provide this ministry, although I suppose it could be argued that one who had Henderson's first two characteristics (liturgical president and local pastor) but lacked the third (preparation) might also be considered an extraordinary minister.

When may presbyters exercise extraordinary ministry? The conditions seem to be similar to those for other extraordinary ministries, namely, the physical absence of the ordinary minister, or the moral absence of that minister owing to the lack of one or another of the several aspects that make up the definition of ordinary ministry. If, for example, the pastor is the liturgical president of the community but has been unable to prepare the homily, a presbyter who has prepared one may deliver the homily, and thus act as an extraordinary minister.

Something similar applies to deacons. While they may preside at some liturgical celebrations — in which case they could be the ordinary minister of the homily, all other conditions being fulfilled[67] — they are never the president of the liturgical assembly of the Eucharist. Here they must always act as an extraordinary minister.

Deacons are extraordinary ministers in other rites. Their exercise of these ministries may help clarify the conditions necessary for one to serve as an extraordinary minister of the homily during Mass. Deacons, for example, are permitted to witness marriages if a priest is not present.[68] How is it possible for a deacon to witness a marriage during Mass when a priest is present? The response from the Holy See has been that absence of the priest is not a condition for valid witnessing of marriage;[69] or, in other words, the priest can be "morally absent" due to pastoral reasons that argue for the deacon and not the priest to witness the marriage. So, too, pastoral reasons may make the liturgical president at the Eucharist "morally absent" when it comes time to deliver the homily.

By definition, the homily is restricted to a bishop, presbyter, or deacon. Even the exceptions that permit lay preaching in church today are carefully phrased to indicate that when lay persons preach, they are not giving a homily on their own. At most they explain the Scriptures or read a homily approved by the pastor. Despite this caution in the documents for the universal Church, it is still legitimate to raise the question of lay persons serving as extraordinary ministers of the homily at Mass. Not only is it clear from an authoritative commentary that the official position of the Apostolic See was not intended to rule out this possibility, but there is also an important precedent where it has been provided for in particular law.

As you may be aware, the dioceses of West Germany held a General Synod from 1972 to 1975.[70] This was a significant effort to involve the whole Church at various levels in exploring the implications of post-Vatican II Catholicism in that country. One of the major factors in pastoral life in Germany, and increasingly nearly everywhere, is the shortage of clergy. To provide for more adequate pastoral care and to assure more effective preaching in a country with a sizeable number of well-educated, theologically literate lay persons, the Synod recommended that the bishops of Germany obtain permission for lay persons to preach, even as homilists. The bishops sent a request to the Congregation for the Clergy, the Vatican office responsible for catechetics and preaching, and received a favorable response on November 20, 1973.[71] Permission was granted for a four-year experimental period, and was extended on June 1, 1977, for an additional four-year period.[72]

Due to delays in starting the practice and other difficulties, evaluations of this experience are not readily available. But the legal precedent is what interests us here. The Roman document included permission for lay persons to give the homily as extraordinary ministers during Mass when the celebrant is "physically or morally" impeded from discharging this office.

The practice of lay persons serving as extraordinary ministers of the homily is also widespread in various mission countries, although documentation for it is sparse.[73] From my own experience I know of situations where the priest travels to various mission stations to celebrate the Eucharist, but catechists he has trained beforehand deliver the homily in the native tongue. It is more than translation. In some areas the priest does not provide any initial commentary on the gospel during the Mass but leaves this responsibility entirely to the catechist. The catechist is accustomed to delivering homilies on Sundays when he has to lead the community worship because the priest does not come to the village.

What will become of the legal precedent from particular law for Germany and from the custom that has developed in various parts of the Church as the revised Code takes effect? I cannot say what will happen factually, but let me comment on the legal aspects of the question.

3. The homily under the revised Code

There is an obligation to provide a homily at all Masses at which the people are present on Sundays and holy days of obligation. It is also a strongly encouraged practice to provide a homily at Masses at which the people are present during the week, especially during Advent and Lent. It is the responsibility of the pastor or rector of the church to see that these provisions are observed.[74] This obligation responds to the right of the people to have the Word of God preached to them and explained for them. The basis for the need to provide a homily is not a question of clerical prerogative but of a Christian right to hear the gospel.[75]

The revised Code clearly distinguishes preaching by lay persons in church from the homily.[76] The homily is by definition something reserved to priests (bishops and presbyters) and deacons and is part of the liturgy itself. It would seem from the wording of this canon that previous indults such as those in Germany would cease to have effect,[77] although new exceptions to this law could be sought by local episcopal conferences or even individual bishops, just as the German bishops did back in the 1970's.

Is that the only option? It seems to me a careful reading of the canons provides another possibility as well. Given the exceptions already built into current liturgical norms, and given the fact that they are carefully phrased to avoid mentioning the activity of lay persons as actually giving a "homily," I believe it can be argued that the term "homily" has become a technical term attached to what a priest or deacon does, and not a restrictive term describing what actually happens during a liturgy.

This is what I mean. All preaching is defined in the revised Code as proposing to the faithful what they must believe and do for the glory of God and salvation of human persons.[78] There is nothing to keep such preaching from being based on the sacred texts, and indeed announcing the Word of God is supposed to be based on the Scripture, tradition, the liturgy, and so on.[79] The words spoken, the doctrine taught, and the message communicated by a lay person preaching in church and by a priest or deacon delivering a homily in that same church building during the Eucharist could be identical. They probably should be at least similar if the preaching of either is to meet the standard for preaching set down in the revised Code. What makes them different?

There are two possibilities. One is that the homily presented by the priest or deacon is done during a liturgical celebration, is part of the liturgy itself, and therefore its context differentiates it from what a lay person does. But how does that distinguish what a lay person may do after the gospel in Masses for children? While it is not termed a "homily," it is supposed to do the same thing the one presiding would do if he could relate to the minds of children.[80] All preaching, according to the revised Code, is supposed to be adapted to the condition of the hearers and the needs of the times.[81]

The other possibility is that we have here an example of a nominalistic definition, that is, the activity is termed "homily" when done by a priest or deacon, "preaching" when done by a lay person. I believe that this is the root distinction we are dealing with in this case. Whether or not the "homily" is a technical term for what a priest or deacon does, is it possible to replace the homily at Mass with what a lay person does when he or she preaches in church? The answer to this must begin with a careful reading of the revised Code on the obligation to provide a homily.

The revised text of the introduction to the Lectionary states that on the prescribed days "there must be a homily in all Masses celebrated with a congregation, even Masses on the preceding evening."[82] How binding is this? The revised Code provides a clause typical of the Church's law: the homily is not to be omitted "nisi gravi de causa" — without a grave reason.[83] What might a grave reason be?

Clearly, physical necessities constitute a grave reason. But so, too, do moral necessities in the Church's legal tradition. If there is a moral impossibility for a priest to witness a marriage — for example, because the civil law forbids him to do so — he should still be present for the celebration of the marriage in the so-called "extraordinary form."[84] He is morally absent even though physically present. There is a grave reason for him to be morally absent, and yet reason too for the couple to proceed with their marriage.

We have seen something similar earlier in the instance of preaching by deacons as extraordinary ministers, or even in the case of their witnessing marriages in the physical presence of a priest, something they are not supposed to do unless a priest is absent. Pastoral need can constitute grave cause in these situations.

The provisions of the permission the German bishops obtained for lay preaching, indeed for lay persons to give the homily at Mass, are quite similar. The celebrant need not be physically impeded from delivering the homily. A lay person may do so even if the celebrant is only morally impeded. Lay persons can also give the homily if they have special competence and would be able to provide an especially opportune exhortation on a special occasion.[85]

Could not these provisions be used to clarify the "grave reason" for which a homily by the ordinary minister (that is, the ordained liturgical president who is also pastor and properly prepared) or even by the ordained extraordinary minister might be omitted on occasion? I think so, and I believe I stand on good canonical grounds in taking this position if one looks to the provisions of the law for clarifying unclear provisions of the Code, both the old and the revised.[86]

Let me sum up my argument this way. From a careful reading of the revised Code, it seems that a lay person could on occasion preach in place of the ordinary or extraordinary minister (an ordained priest or deacon) who would usually provide a homily. The conditions under which this could be done would depend on the physical or moral unavailability of the ordained ordinary or extraordinary minister and could arise from pastoral need.

Who is responsible to judge whether and when this may be done? The revised Code provides three levels of competence in this matter. First, the diocesan bishop is to issue norms regulating preaching in the diocese.[87] Second, it is up to pastors and rectors of churches to see that a homily is provided.[88] It would also seem to be up to them to ensure that appropriate preaching is provided when grave cause keeps them from assuring a technical homily on the days required or at other times. Finally, the episcopal conference may establish norms to govern lay preaching in the country.[89]

To summarize the import of this section:

1. Since Vatican II, the legal basis for preaching has shifted from jurisdiction to baptism, by which the baptized participate in Christ's *munus docendi.*[90]

2. All the baptized are encouraged—indeed, have the responsibility and the mission—to proclaim the gospel in the world.[91]

3. Although the 1917 Code prohibits authorizing lay persons, including religious, to preach in church, the law since Vatican II has made a number of exceptions to the rule. The revision of the Code reverses the prohibition, permitting authorization of lay persons to preach in church presumably in the name of the Church.[92]

4. This authorization does not include the homily, which in law is defined as what a priest or deacon does as part of the liturgy. It can be omitted on required days only for grave cause.[93] If omitted for such a cause, preeminent among which could be pastoral reasons, I suggest it could be replaced on those occasions with preaching by a lay person.

III. Looking Toward the Future

I have no crystal ball. I cannot assure you that the interpretation I have just proposed will meet with general acceptance or even be implemented in practice. But I believe a few comments about the future may be in order.

First, there is a question of method, or how the question of lay preaching is to be posed canonically. I have used the traditional exegetical approach, searching in the exceptions the way current and proposed law can be interpreted to open as wide a field of possibilities for lay preaching as possible. Other methods could be used. Certainly in this country a more popular approach would be to base a canonical study on rights — the right of the Christian community and of all people to have the gospel preached to them or even the personal right claimed by individuals to preach. Personally, I believe that the argument from the right to hear the gospel is more congenial to the current canonical theories on rights.[94] But I must admit that a good case can be based on the individual's right to preach, beginning with the Vatican II assertion that from charisms there arise rights and duties in the Church as well as within the world.[95]

What method should be adopted depends in large part on which one is more effective, that is, effective in achieving the end rather than merely effective in venting our emotions. There is, furthermore, the fact of politics. Politics is the "art of the possible," and this concept is no stranger to the Church or to members of this audience.

I have noted the cautious openings to lay preaching present in the revised Code. If these are to amount to anything, we must be better, or certainly more effective, politicians in the Church at large than the party of Innocent III were. Otherwise there could well be a significant backlash to this aspect of the revised Code, or at least a non-reception of it.

Moreover, the revised Code will not be self-implementing. It dares to take the risk of being a law for disciples, reduces the mandatory elements in the law, and relies on local legislation to put it to work. The process for implementing the Code is a good example of how politics can be of service in expanding lay preaching and in putting the Church in a position more faithful to its theological premises.

To participate in synods, councils, committees, etc., takes

time, patience, and solid homework. That's work. Are we willing to undertake that kind of work? The answer will determine the extent to which our generation will contribute to the Church's effort to become more faithful to the gospel.

Let me add a note of caution on politics. From Father Schillebeeckx's paper and other historical studies, it is clear that we can be victimized by other people's political battles — seculars versus monks or mendicants, popes versus bishops, or even charismatic ministry versus professional ministry. In the highly charged political atmosphere of the Church today, we must avoid acting naïvely or like babes in the woods if the cause of lay preaching is to be served.

Finally, there is the opportunity of praxis. It does little good to lobby for lay preaching if there are none to preach. Three elements are already possible, and each is a challenging discipline.

First, adequate preparation for preaching begins with sensitivity to the Word through *vita apostolica* and serious study.

Next there must be a genuine sensitivity to the community. Those who would preach must know their audiences and share their experiences to whatever extent possible.

Finally, all those options of evangelization, catechesis, and preaching that are already open must be used to the full. To proclaim good news to a frightened and broken world, to call even the Church to constant conversion, and to announce the gospel are ministries already open to all. The experience, example, and confidence of doing preaching may, in the last analysis, be what expands lay preaching most effectively.

NOTES

1. John XXIII, Solemn Allocution to Cardinals in Rome, January 25, 1959: *Acta Apostolicae Sedis* (hereafter AAS) 51 (1959) 65–69.

2. See Francis G. Morrisey, "The Spirit of Canon Law, Teaching of Paul VI," *Origins* 8 (1978) 34–40.

3. *Codex iuris canonici,* canons 2, 13, 25. Hereafter the Code will be cited thus: CIC and the canon number.

4. The revised Code was promulgated by Pope John Paul II on January 25, 1983, to take effect November 27, 1983, the first Sunday of Advent. It will be cited in this article thus: '83 CIC.

5. See CIC 1323, 1326. In the CIC, the pope's primacy of jurisdiction is defined as applying to faith and morals as well as to discipline and governance (CIC 218, S1), and he obtains this immediately upon acceptance of legitimate election (CIC 219), even though he may not yet be ordained to sacred orders. In effect, magisterium depends on jurisdiction, and in the Code jurisdiction is independent of sacramental participation by ordination in the *munera* of Christ.

Bishops, likewise, begin to exercise magisterium in virtue of their office from the moment they take canonical possession of it, even though they have not yet been consecrated (CIC 334, 336). At Vatican II, efforts were made to change this by rooting the power of bishops (and pope) in sacramental consecration.

The issue, however, remains debated. See Wilhelm Bertrams, *Quaestiones fundamentales iuris canonici* (Rome: Pontificia Universita Gregoriana, 1969), who continues to emphasize the role of the pope as crucial to exercising power even under Vatican II teaching; Klaus Mörsdorf, "Kanonische Recht als theologische Disziplin," *Archiv für katholisches Kirchenrecht* 145 (1976) 45–58, who holds that the Council reversed the Code's position and rooted all sacred power in the sacrament of orders; and Edward J. Kilmartin, "Lay Participation in the Apostolate of the Hierarchy," *The Jurist* 41 (1981) 343–370, who proposes to base the discussion more on the Trinity as a way out of the theoretical impasse.

6. CIC 107: "Ex divina institutione sunt in Ecclesia *clerici* a *laicis* distincti" (emphasis in original); CIC 948: "Ordo ex Christi institutione clericos a laicis in Ecclesia distinguit ad fidelium regimen et cultus divini ministerium."

7. See CIC 1323, 1326.

8. CIC 1327–1408.

9. CIC 1342, S2.

10. Vatican II, Dogmatic Constitution on the Church, *Lumen gentium* (hereafter LG) 32.

11. Vatican II, Dogmatic Constitution on Divine Revelation, *Dei Verbum*, 7-10.

12. LG 12, 33; Vatican II, Decree on the Apostolate of the Laity, "Apostolicam actuositatem" (hereafter AA) 3.

13. LG 10, 32.

14. LG 30.

15. Paul VI, Address to the Commission for the Revision of the Code, November 20, 1965: AAS 57 (1965) 988.

16. '83 CIC 747-833.

17. '83 CIC 756-759.

18. '83 CIC 756-759.

19. Paul VI, Apostolic Exhortation *Evangelii nuntiandi* (December 8, 1975).

20. '83 CIC 760.

21. '83 CIC 756-759.

22. '83 CIC 758, 759, 766.

23. '83 CIC 763.

24. '83 CIC 764.

25. '83 CIC 762; LG 25; Vatican II, Decree on the Ministry and Life of Priests, *Presbyterorum ordinis*, 4.

26. '83 CIC 766.

27. '83 CIC 768.

28. '83 CIC 769.

29. '83 CIC 772, 770.

30. '83 CIC 767.

31. See J. H. Nichols, "Les laïcs et l'annonce de la parole de Dieu," *Nouvelle revue theologique* 93 (1971) 821-848; James H. Provost, "Laity in the Pulpit," *America* 141/17 (December 1, 1979) 347-348; Maureen Carroll and Kathleen Cannon, "Enfleshing the Word: The Case for Lay Preachers," *Liturgy* 24/3 (May-June, 1979) 31-34; John A. Gurrieri, "The Homily: The State of the Question – Again," *Living Light* 17 (1980) 164-170; J. Frank Henderson, "The Minister of Liturgical Preaching," *Worship* 56 (1982) 214-230.

32. LG 25.

33. See Paul VI, *Evangelii nuntiandi* 59; John Paul II, Apostolic Exhortation *Catechesi tradendae* (October 16, 1979) 16.

34. See William Skudlarek, "Assertion Without Knowledge: The Lay Preaching Controversy of the High Middle Ages" (Ph.D. diss., Princeton Theological Seminary, 1976; Ann Arbor, Mich.: University Microfilms, 1980); Elissa A. Rinere, "Authorization for Lay Preaching in the Church" (J.C.L. diss., The Catholic University of America, 1981).

35. LG 31, 33; AA 6; Vatican II, Decree on the Church's Missionary Activity, *Ad gentes* (hereafter AG) 17.

36. CIC 1328.

37. CIC 467, 1350, S1; Vatican II, Decree on the Bishops' Pastoral Office in the Church, *Christus Dominus*, 30; S. Congregation for Divine Worship, *Rite of Christian Initiation of Adults* (hereafter RCIA), January 6, 1972, nos. 13, 16, 45.

38. CIC 1341.

39. '83 CIC 764.

40. See CIC 1342.

41. RCIA, "Introduction," especially no. 48.

42. CIC 1333.

43. See John Paul II, *Catechesi tradendae* 66-69.

44. See Paul VI, Motu Proprio *Ministeria quaedam* (August 15, 1972) IV; S. Congregation for Divine Worship, *Institution of Lectors and Acolytes* (December 3, 1972): "Institution of Lectors," 4.

45. S. Congregation for Divine Worship, Instruction *Liturgicae instaurationes* (September 5, 1970) 3(f); S. Congregation for the Sacraments and Divine Worship, *Lectionary for Mass*, 2nd editio typica (January 21, 1981): "Introduction," 15.

46. S. Congregation of Rites, Instruction *Inter Oecumenici* (September 26, 1964) 37.

47. S. Congregation for Divine Worship, *Liturgicae instaurationes* 6(e).

48. S. Congregation for Divine Worship, Decree on Holy Communion and Worship of the Eucharist Outside Mass (June 21, 1973) 91, 95.

49. S. Congregation for Divine Worship, *Directory for Masses with Children* (November 1, 1973) 24.

50. '83 CIC 766.

51. S. Congregation of Rites, *Inter Oecumenici* 54.

52. *Ibid.*, 52.

53. See the discussion in Gurrieri and Henderson, cited above in note 31.

54. S. Congregation for the Sacraments and Divine Worship, *Lectionary*, 24; '83 CIC 767, S1.

55. RCIA, 92, 138, 185, 190-191; S. Congregation for Divine Worship, *Rite of Confirmation* (August 22, 1971) 39; S. Congregation for Divine Worship, *Rite of Penance* (December 2, 1973) 52; S. Congregation for Divine Worship, Decree on Holy Communion and Worship of the Eucharist Outside Mass, 29; S. Congregation for Divine Worship, *Rite of Funerals* (August 15, 1969) 64.

56. See Henderson, "The Minister of Liturgical Preaching," for a careful analysis.

57. S. Congregation for Divine Worship, *Christian Initiation: "General Introduction"* (n.d.), 16; Decree on Holy Communion and Worship of the Eucharist Outside Mass, 17.

58. CIC 197, S1; '83 CIC 131, S1.

59. *Lectionary*, 52.

60. S. Congregation for Divine Worship, *The Sacramentary* (March 26, 1970) 42.

61. Reply of the Pontifical Commission for the Interpretation of the Decrees of the Second Vatican Council, January 11, 1971; AAS 63 (1971) 329; *Canon Law Digest* (hereafter CLD) 7:633.

62. V. Carbone, "De commissione decretis Concilii Vaticani Secundi interpretandis: Dubiorum solutionum explanatio," *Monitor ecclesiasticus* 97 (1972) 323–327.

63. Henderson, 218.

64. *Ibid.*, 219.

65. *Ibid.*, 218.

66. *Ibid.*, 221.

67. See Bishops' Committee on the Liturgy, *Study Text VI: The Deacon, Minister of Word and Sacrament* (Washington: USCC Publications, 1979) 46–47.

68. Paul VI, Motu Proprio *Sacrum diaconatus ordinem* (June 18, 1967) 22, 4°.

69. Reply of the Pontifical Commission for the Interpretation of the Decrees of the Second Vatican Council, April 4, 1969; AAS 61 (1969) 348; CLD 7:134

70. *Gemeinsame Synode der Bistümer in der Bundesrepublik Deutschland*, 2 vols. (Freiburg i. Breisgau: Herder, 1976–1977).

71. Reply of the S. Congregation for the Clergy, November 20, 1973: CLD 8:941–944.

72. Reply of the S. Congregation for the Clergy, June 1, 1977, prot. n. 155481/I.

73. The practice was obviously known to the Fathers of the Second Vatican Council – see AG 16.

74. '83 CIC 767, SS2–4.

75. '83 CIC 213.

76. '83 CIC 766: ". . . et salvo can. 767 S1."

77. '83 CIC 6, S1.

78. '83 CIC 768, S1.

79. '83 CIC 760.

80. S. Congregation for Divine Worship, *Directory for Masses with Children*, 24.

81. '83 CIC 769.

82. *Lectionary*, 25.

83. '83 CIC 767, S2.

84. CIC 1098; '83 CIC 1116.

85. Reply of the S. Congregation for the Clergy, November 20, 1973, 2(c); CLD 8:943.

86. CIC 18, 20; '83 CIC 17, 19.

87. '83 CIC 772, S1.

88. '83 CIC 767, S4.

89. '83 CIC 766.

90. LG 12.

91. AA 3.

92. CIC 1342; '83 CIC 766.

93. '83 CIC 767.

94. See Alvaro del Portillo, *Fieles y laicos en la Iglesia* (Pamplona: EUNSA, 1969); '83 CIC 747.

95. AA 3.

APPENDIX

Homily

October 9, 1982

JOAN DELAPLANE, O.P.

(The homily at the Liturgy of the Word was based on the Scripture readings designated in the Lectionary for this day: Galatians 3:22-29 and Luke 11:27-29.)

From Paul, called by the will of God to be an apostle of Christ Jesus, to the people of God from the churches of thirty-five States in America, and from Canada, assembled in Columbus, Ohio:

Grace to you, and peace from God our Father and the Lord Jesus.

I understand that you are gathered here on this ninth day of October, of the year of our Lord 1982, to discuss an issue of great urgency for the Church: the mission to preach the Good News of our Lord Jesus Christ.

Much of the heart of that Good News you just heard read to you in my letter to the Galatians: "All baptized in Christ, you have all clothed yourselves in Christ, and there are no more distinctions; you are all one in Christ Jesus."

You are all one in Christ Jesus! There is the awesome truth! Now, I firmly believed that when it was first revealed to me; I am not certain, however, that I understood all that would be involved in trying to live it out. It was that first part — no longer Jew nor Greek — to which I directed so much of my energies. You must know how I anguished; how I traveled to Jerusalem; how I confronted Peter at Antioch until he was finally able to say: "I realized then that God was giving them the identical thing he gave to us when we believed in the Lord Jesus, and who was I to stand in God's way?" (Acts 11:17).

Dealing with the reality that there was no longer any distinction between Jew and Greek — we were all one in Christ Jesus — was, I believe, the first real trauma of the early Church. Can you appreciate for just a few minutes how very difficult and emotional it was for the Church to embrace that truth? For hundreds of years we Jewish males had given thanks daily that we were not born Gentiles, slaves, or women. By faith and baptism in Christ Jesus, however, all distinctions of class, race, and sex are dissolved. "And for anyone who is in Christ, there is a new creation; the old creation has gone, and now the new one is here" (2 Cor 5:17).

How hard a time I had to convince even Peter of the way we needed to drastically change our attitudes, our outlook and customs, and, yes, even our long tradition of laws, if we were to be true to the Lord Jesus and embody and enflesh this truth in the community. Why do we creatures of the law find it so hard to accept the freedom offered us in Christ Jesus? We can know with the head; it is quite another thing to live it out, isn't it? Peter ate with the Gentiles a few times, but when the pressure was on him from some of the others, he backed off. I guess it's understandable when we remember that for two thousand years we Jews found our identity as the chosen ones, the elect of God. We avoided any contact with the *goyim*, the heathen Gentiles. We obeyed the long list of rules and regulations, were circumcised, and adhered to the Torah.

Is it really surprising, then, that there was so much contention, confusion, and unrest regarding this issue? We had to grapple with our new understanding that "Anyone who is convinced that he belongs to Christ, must go on to reflect that we all belong to Christ no less than he does" (2 Cor 10:7). Some found it harder than others; it was like having a rug pulled out from under them. Their whole basis for identity was shaken. But the new dispensation in the Lord Jesus can be understood no other way. There is a new order of existence. One's identity now by faith and baptism is in putting on Christ, which necessarily involves the collapse of any walls of distinction of race or class or sex. As hard as it was for us Jews, we had to let go of any elitism; we had to accept the chosenness of all people before the Lord.

It took almost one thousand nine hundred years before the followers of the Way began to address the second part of that truth: there is no longer slave nor free. And are there not yet some who, because of their race, assume a superior stance? And now you are beginning to look at the third part: there is no longer male nor female. With that issue, the Church of the twentieth century is probably facing its second real trauma. Once again, the issue involves a deeply rooted emotional and cultural conditioning. Are there not yet some who claim by word or action an elitism based on sex?

We Jews were sincerely and firmly convinced of our chosenness, based on religious convictions, no less; but Jesus revealed another reality. So, too, race and sex elitism have been, for some, deeply rooted in their own sincere religious conviction; again, Jesus has revealed another reality.

Those who walked with Jesus said that he referred to the Torah, where it is written: "God said, 'Let us make man in our own image, in the likeness of ourselves, and let them be masters of the fish of the sea, the birds of heaven, the cattle, all the wild beasts and all the reptiles that crawl upon the earth.' . . . in the image of God he created him, male and female he created them" (Gen 1:26-27). Here we have the heart of how Jesus perceived the dignity and equality of male and female. Jesus was an observant Jew, a rabbi; but his attitude toward women was very countercultural. Just as in the political sphere he did not organize and undo the oppressive Roman rule, neither did he perceive his mission to undo the social structures of his times. But his life, his words, and his actions laid the principles of dignity and equality of all for his followers to build upon.

Jesus' own faith-experience of himself as Beloved Son of the

Father rooted his identity, and that rootedness freed him to relate comfortably with all persons. He respected each one as also a beloved daughter and son of that same Father. Any laws that did not seem to respect this dignity and equality Jesus, apparently, had no problem negating. He taught Mary, even when her sister was upset. He touched the woman suffering with hemorrhage; and, contrary to law, he did not undergo any ritual of purification. He dialogued with the woman at the well. He affirmed women who ministered to him by financial resources and by anointing. Most particularly, he revealed his risen self to a woman, and, contrary to tradition, missioned Mary: "Go to my brothers and tell them for me, I go back up to him who is my Father and your Father, my God and your God" (John 20:17-18).

Unlike many of the Jews of his day, Jesus saw the dignity of woman, not in her physical functions, not in the fact that she could bear "sons of Abraham"; but, like his mother, persons were to be praised and exalted for hearing the Word of God and keeping it. In the new creation, therein lies one's greatness.

In the new dispensation you are all one in Christ Jesus. The variety of gifts — preaching, teaching, healing, administration — "all these are the work of one and the same Spirit who distributes different gifts to different people just as the Spirit chooses" (1 Cor 12:11). All are called to use their gifts for the building up of the Body of Christ. What is important is that "Christ is proclaimed; and in that I rejoice" (Phil 1:18).

Though I will admit my ambivalence at times regarding the role of women in the early Church, you know that even then I highly regarded my female co-workers Prisca, Phoebe, Junia, and many others. "The entire creation is groaning in one great act of giving birth"; and, as you might say it in your age, it ought to be by the Lamaze method. Men and women must labor together in the field and in the birthing of the new creation as did my friends Prisca and Aquila. The power of God's Word must be unleashed by women and men alike who have been gifted by the Spirit, or the Church will be impoverished.

"All baptized in Christ, you have all clothed yourselves in Christ, and there are no more distinctions; you are all one in Christ Jesus." I, Paul, poured out my energies in the early Christian community to bring to embodiment the truth that there is no more Jew nor Greek. The challenge before you of the twentieth century is to continue to pray, preach, confront, hope, and love the Church into the full enfleshment of no longer slave nor free, male nor female. Someday, by the power of the Spirit of the Risen Jesus in our midst, it will be said of slaves and of women as was said of Gentiles: "I realized then that God was giving them the identical thing he gave to us when we believed in the Lord Jesus, and who was I to stand in God's way?" (Acts 11:17).

"Finally, my brothers and sisters, farewell. All the saints greet you. The grace of the Lord Jesus Christ and the love of God and the fellowship of the Holy Spirit be with you all" (2 Cor 13:11-14).

THE CONTRIBUTORS

Edward Schillebeeckx, o.p., is Professor of Theology and the History of Theology at the University of Nijmegen in The Netherlands. He served as a *peritus* for Vatican Council II and is an editorial director of *Concilium*, as well as a frequent contributor. His international reputation as a dogmatic theologian has been enhanced in recent years by his works: *Jesus: An Experiment in Christology* (1979) and *Christ: The Experience of Christ as Lord* (1982), two parts of a planned trilogy; as well as by the provocative study *Ministry, Leadership in the Community of Jesus Christ*.

William J. Hill, o.p., is Professor of Systematic Theology at The Catholic University of America, Washington, D.C. He holds an S.T.D. from The University of St. Thomas in Rome and is a former member of the faculty of the Dominican House of Studies in Washington, D.C. He has been editor-in-chief of *The Thomist* and has served on the editorial board of the *New Catholic Encyclopedia, Communio,* and *Listening.* His published works include *Knowing the Unknown God* and *The Three-Personed God,* as well as numerous articles in various theological journals. He is a past president of The Catholic Theological Society of America and currently Catholic delegate to the Bilateral Consultations between the Roman Catholic Church and the Reformed/Presbyterian Churches.

Sandra M. Schneiders, i.h.m., is Associate Professor of New Testament Studies and Spirituality at the Jesuit School of Theology/Graduate Theological Union, Berkeley, California. She is also on the staff of the Institute for Spirituality and Worship at the Jesuit School. Her writings include books on spiritual direction and on the resurrection narrative in John's Gospel as well as numerous articles in professional and pastoral journals. She is a member of the religious congregation of the Sisters, Servants of the Immaculate Heart of Mary, Monroe, Michigan.

Mary Collins, o.s.b., is Associate Professor in the School of Religious Studies, The Catholic University of America, Washington, D.C. She teaches and writes on the relationship between liturgy and culture. An associate editor of *Worship* and a member of the editorial board of *Concilium*, she has published in those journals as well as in *The Jurist* and *The Living Light,* and has contributed essays to several collections. She is a member of the Benedictine Sisters, Atchison, Kansas.

James H. Provost is Associate Professor of Canon Law at The Catholic University of America, Washington, D.C., and the Executive Coordinator of the Canon Law Society of America. A graduate of Carroll

College in Helena, Montana, he holds S.T.B. and M.A. degrees from the University of Louvain (Belgium) and a J.C.D. from the Lateran University in Rome. He served as Chancellor and Officialis of the Diocese of Helena from 1967 to 1979, is a past president of the Canon Law Society of America, and currently serves as managing editor of *The Jurist*.

MAUREEN P. CARROLL, O.P., is a doctoral candidate in Systematic Theology at The Catholic University of America, Washington, D.C. Her dissertation, *A Foundation for a Theology of Christian Conversion*, makes extensive use of Schillebeeckx's hermeneutics of historical experience and supplements this with a contemporary reconsideration of Aquinas's doctrine of the gifts of the Holy Spirit in the lives of the faithful. She has written and spoken on preaching by the non-ordained in connection with her theological and personal interests in women in Christian tradition; and her "Homily for the Feast of Teresa of Avila, Doctor of the Church" appears in the collection *Spinning a Sacred Yarn: Women Speak from the Pulpit* (1982).

DONALD GOERGEN, O.P., is a Dominican priest and a systematic theologian. He is the author of *The Sexual Celibate* and *The Power of Love*. He was formerly Professor of Christology and Spirituality at Aquinas Institute, now located in St. Louis. He resides currently in Madison, Wisconsin, where he is engaged full time in research in the area of Christology.

MARY CATHERINE HILKERT, O.P., a member of the Sisters of St. Dominic of Akron, Ohio, is a doctoral candidate in the Theology Department at The Catholic University of America, Washington, D.C. At the present time, she is writing her dissertation, entitled *Towards a Theology of Proclamation*, using Edward Schillebeeckx's hermeneutics of tradition as a foundation for a theology of proclamation. She received her M.A. from The Catholic University of America in 1979 and has been a lecturer in the Department of Theology there in the area of Revelation and Faith. Sister Mary Catherine has given workshops on preaching, has preached retreats, and has published in *Homily Service*.

WILLIAM SKUDLAREK, O.S.B., is Dean and Rector of the School of Theology, St. John's University, Collegeville, Minnesota. He holds a Ph.D. in Homiletics from Princeton Theological Seminary. His doctoral dissertation addressed the lay preaching controversy in the High Middle Ages, concentrating especially on the reaction of Innocent III to the Waldensian and Franciscan movements.

KATHLEEN CANNON, O.P., has chaired the Religious Studies Department at Albertus Magnus College in New Haven, Connecticut, where she taught courses in Scripture and Theology. She has taught Biblical Preaching at Wesley Methodist Seminary in Washington, D.C., and at the Princeton Theological Seminary. She prepared her Doctor of Ministry degree at The Catholic University of America with a study of preaching and the non-ordained. She is a regular contributor to *Homily Service*. Sister Kathleen is a member of the St. Mary of the Springs congregation of Dominican Sisters in Columbus, Ohio.

JOAN DELAPLANE, O.P., an Adrian Dominican Sister, is currently Assistant Professor of Homiletics at Aquinas Institute in St. Louis. She received her M.A. in English and M.A. in Religious Studies from the University of Detroit, her M. Div. from SS. Cyril and Methodius Seminary, Orchard Lake, Michigan, and has done graduate study in Guidance and Counselling at Michigan State University. She has had wide experience in preaching and directing retreats and has directed preaching workshops for Catholic clergy and Protestant ministers.

NADINE FOLEY, O.P., is currently Assistant Professor of Philosophy at Marist College, Poughkeepsie, New York. She is a former vicaress of the Adrian Dominican Sisters and former chairperson of the Dominican Leadership Conference. She holds a Ph.D. in Philosophy from The Catholic University of America and an S.T.M. from Union Theological Seminary, New York. She has had a wide range of ministerial experience and has lectured and written on mission, ministry, and women in the Church.